Front Cover: *The Gallery overlooking Gibraltar at the Yorkshire Evening News Tournament*

Inside front cover: *The Centenary Captain, Jamie Allison, drives in before the members and past captains*

Inside back cover: *The Cenentary Captain, Vice Captain and Lady Captain with 21 Past Captains at the Centenary Captain's Drive in*

Back cover: *Spectators at the Gibraltar Day event with Dr Mackenzie's famous hole in the background.*

ACKNOWLEDGEMENTS

We would like to thank the many organisations and individuals who contributed and provided photographs reproduced in this book, particularly:

- Stewart Laws • Geoff Talbott • Margaret Calvert • Bob Adcock
- David Earnshaw • Andrew Blackburn • Ken Myers • Gerry Connolly
- Albert Geoffrey Parker • Bryon Hutchinson • Martin Heggie • Mollie Midwood
- Adele Allen • Jamie Allison • Vince Green • Ron Brown • Sid Bowyer
- John Lawson-Brown • Peter Rogerson • Victor Watson • David Sheret
- Jean Burrows • John Murtland • Steven Robinson • John Wilson
- Suzie Cowling • Heaney & Mill • Golf Illustrated • Tom Watson • Peter Alliss
- Marco Pierre White • Simon Golding of SGTV • Getty Images
- Cypress Point Club • World Golf Hall of Fame • Yorkshire Evening News
- Hields Aviation • MacKenzie Golf Society Clubs
- Jack Nicklaus photo, courtesy Jim Mandeville/Nicklaus Companies
- Red Kite photo, courtesy of Mike Ashforth, Yorkshire Red Kite Project

All other illustrations originate from material belonging to the club. While every effort has been made to trace copyright material used in this book, some sources have been impossible to track down. We will be pleased to hear from anyone who feels that their material has not been given due acknowledgement so that this may be rectified in any future edition and we apologise for any inadvertent breach of their copyright.

DEDICATIONS

To Lindsay Rogerson and Judi Talbott for their tolerance and forbearance.
To David Sheret and his Committee for their encouragement and support.

Copyright © The Moortown Golf Club Ltd.

Printed and bound by Deanprint Limited,
Cheadle Heath Works, Stockport Road, Cheshire SK3 0PR

CONTENTS

Acknowledgements		1
Contents		2
Introduction		3
Chapter I	The Foundation	4
Chapter II	Dr Alister MacKenzie	10
Chapter III	The First 50 Years	18
Chapter IV	The Course	26
Chapter V	The Clubhouse	38
Chapter VI	Professionals, Greens & Clubhouse Staff	44
Chapter VII	1929 Ryder Cup	52
Chapter VIII	Professional Tournaments & Championships	62
Chapter IX	Amateur Tournaments	72
Chapter X	Club Team Matches	80
Chapter XI	The MacKenzie Cup	86
Chapter XII	Millennium Festival Week	94
Chapter XIII	The Ladies	102
Chapter XIV	Visitors & Visits	116
Chapter XV	Club Trophies & Champions	122
Chapter XVI	Club Happenings	128
Chapter XVII	The Centenary Celebrations	134
Chapter XVIII	Officers of the Club	150
Chapter XIX	Flora & Fauna	154
Chapter XX	What the Players Say	158

INTRODUCTION

Sidney H. Warnes compiled a brief document in 1959 entitled 'Moortown Golf Club 1909-1959' to mark the club's Jubilee Celebrations. Thirty-one years later, Ron Brown, the then Club Secretary, updated the Jubilee history and in 1990 produced a handsome leatherbound manuscript typed book. Ten years later Ron's work was re-published as part of Moortown's landmark celebration of the Millennium.

This centenary book, produced for the benefit of all the club's members and its friends, is the latest of Moortown's historical publications and it has drawn heavily on Ron Brown's work.

Meanwhile in 2006 Margaret Calvert, a very active lady member of 65 years standing, began to research the history of the Ladies' section. Having extracted a number of amusing and interesting items from the club's minutes, Margaret produced her own book entitled "Ladies Golf at Moortown from 1909" which, with some minor modifications, has been incorporated into this book.

These publications have been two key sources of material for this centenary book which has been compiled by Peter Rogerson, a past captain and chairman of the club. He has drawn, too, from additional material quarried from the club's own archives in order to chronicle an extensive illustrated history up to 2009. Geoff Talbott, a journalist friend and former Managing Editor of BBC Radio Leeds, and latterly the BBC TV's Northern Regional Political Editor - and a keen supporter of Moortown Golf Club - has edited the content for your enjoyment.

In a relatively short time span Moortown has managed to become famous wherever golf is played – not least because in 1929 it hosted the first Ryder Cup Match on this side of the Atlantic. The many professional and amateur events which have been played here since then testify to its merits. However, much of Moortown's fame can be attributed to the course's design and its reputation as a classic example of golf architecture. The designer was the late Dr Alister MacKenzie who laid out many world famous courses both in this country and in America. Moortown retains many of the features characteristic of his earliest work. This fame in itself deserves significant recognition in this history.

A history like this, if it is to earn the respect of its readers, demands accuracy and comprehensivity. But, with the best will in the world, early records disappear and memories of long-standing members dim and so the record must be written while we are lucky to still possess much of both. It is hoped that this account will do justice to the stalwarts of the past who have brought the club to its present eminence and be of interest to present and future members – the keepers of the flame - as they seek to understand and build upon the history and traditions of Moortown Golf Club.

We hope there are few, but apologise in advance for, any omissions and oversights; unfortunately events at the club are not always recorded, photographed or filed and captioned so that future generations can take advantage of them for publications like this.

Ron Brown, a former secretary and the author of 'Moortown Golf Club 1909 - 1990'

Margaret Calvert, the author of 'Ladies' Golf at Moortown from 1909'

Geoff Talbott and Peter Rogerson, Moortown's Centenary book's editor and compiler respectively

I THE FOUNDATION

In 1903 while on holiday in Bridlington, Frederick Lawson-Brown went to watch the Yorkshire Amateur Golf Championship which was being held nearby at Ganton Golf Club. Ganton was – and still is - noted for its beautiful surroundings. Lawson-Brown quickly fell for its charms. There and then he decided the city of Leeds should have a similar location.

However, little was done to realise this ambition until 1906 when Frederick Lawson-Brown was asked to join a golf club on the Leeds-Wakefield road. He was surprised by the comparison with Ganton and this strengthened his resolve to find a site in the Leeds area which would match its standards. Today, of course, such a major project would bring with it a vast array of golf course architects, advisers, constructors, and planners. Yet Lawson-Brown enlisted the help of just three associates - J R Greenhalgh, H Leach and J H Mountain. None of them were golfers.

Week by week they were out and about reconnoitring suitable land for their golf course. In time they sought out two others who did play golf, F Turner and N Casson of Woodhall Hills. Eight months of visits, meetings and discussions followed - a period which Lawson-Brown described as 'pretty grim' in his personal notes. But in October 1908 they found a site at Black Moor on the northern fringe of the expanding city. It lay five and a half miles from the city centre, though at the time it was outside the boundaries of Leeds. Black Moor was a heathery, boggy hillside, full of stagnant pools, but brim full of potential, too. The moor ran northwards to a stream, and north of the stream was some farmland known as Alwoodley Moss.

The land belonged to the Lane-Fox family, now best known for their country seat at Bramham Park, near Wetherby. But at the turn of the century the Lane Fox estate owned substantial tracts of land in north Leeds, including the former Alwoodley Old Hall which dated back to the 1700s. Much of their land at Black Moor was leased to a farmer called Smith who lived at Mount Farm on Alwoodley Lane. However, the founders made no headway in their approaches to him in an effort to lease the land. As a result contact was made with the agent for the Lane-Fox family, a Mr Harrison. Simultaneously the founders invited Dr Alister Mackenzie to visit the site which he duly did in October 1908; he rapidly came to the conclusion that it would make a fine course and offered to aid the founders in its design. A month later the negotiations with the Lane Fox land agent bore fruit; the necessary land was acquired at a rental of £100 for ten years, free of rates and tax. This was considered a very reasonable figure; other courses had paid considerably more.

Earlier that month a meeting had been held at F J Turner's house where the decision was formally taken to form a golf club. Little reference is made to its name or its derivation. But the first recorded minutes were headed 'Moortown Golf Club'. As the new club was in the Moortown/Alwoodley district and as the Alwoodley Golf Club was already in place, Moortown became the obvious title. Whatever the reason, it was an apt choice because the terrain and the dominance of Black Moor suggested a moorland course with gorse and heather.

Later in November 1908 a second meeting was held at F J Turner's house when it was decided to send out circulars inviting one hundred members to join the new club at a subscription cost of two guineas per person. With the prevailing economic conditions it was anticipated that the probability of attracting further members would be high, even though at that time golf was a minority pursuit and did not have the popular support that it enjoys today.

Fred Lawson-Brown (centre) with a group of golfing friends

Setting out on such a venture beyond the outskirts of the city, well away from peoples' homes and without the benefits of public transport, would seem to be a highly speculative matter. Just getting to the new club required taking public transport to Street Lane corner followed by a walk of over a mile, generally uphill and over rough ground. Notwithstanding the difficulties, the club's founding fathers were steadfast in their convictions.

From those meetings of November 1908 onwards, the pace of progress quickened. Forty seven committee meetings were held, mostly at the Hotel Metropole, between November 1908 and November 1909. The first General Meeting of the original and prospective members was held on the 16th December, 1908, to test the level of support.

The founders need not have worried. The first General Meeting was very well attended and the project was given great support. The first officers were appointed and the first 100 gentlemen and 50 lady members were enrolled at fees of two guineas and one guinea respectively. For those who hate to miss a bargain, life membership was then available at sixteen guineas for a gentleman and twenty-one guineas for a gentleman and his wife. After seven days, the subscription for new entrants was raised to three guineas - one of the quickest subscription increases in Moortown's history.

Most of the original members came from the Chapeltown, Harehills, Roundhay and Moortown districts and their subscriptions were payable from January 1st, 1909, by which time it was hoped that progress would have been made on building the course. The first steps having been taken, the club was officially founded on the 12th January, 1909 when it was incorporated as a limited company.

Early construction of the course, artificial hummock at Moortown constructed from the stones removed from the fairway.

A Course Construction Committee consisting of Dr MacKenzie, F J Turner, C T Ross, and S R Rush was set up to supervise the development of the course. Construction was slow at first as the initial holes were laid out on Black Moor. Drainage proved to be a difficult task. Indeed, subsequent head greenkeepers have found it a recurring problem. Originally, rubble drainage was used, but in time standard land tiles were laid.

The construction of the course turned out to be a popular local attraction. Many came to view the works, usually on Saturday afternoons, anxious to see the progress, though many left feeling certain it would never make a golf course - even in

Original 7th green with Gibraltar in the background

those days, would-be golf course architects were abundant. But the doubters were soon proved wrong. By the summer of 1909 play was possible on nine holes - a feat which today would be considered nigh impossible.

The first hole was the old short fourteenth which offered a gentle downhill start to the round. The second was played up the hedge side to the top of the field where the fifteenth green is now. The third was played to the opposite corner of the same field and the fourth up the same field again, to the front of the present fifteenth green. Three holes in one field certainly put the land to good use and must have been testimony to the straightness of the golfers' play. The fifth hole was the present sixteenth and was called the 'Holly Bush' hole. The holly bush in front of the present sixteenth tee which has now been removed, created, as it grew, a potential problem for those wishing to align their tee shots to the right hand side of the fairway. Nor was it popular for the green keepers who wished to use the full extent of the tee. Its shape and height was the subject of keen debate at a meeting of the Green Committee.

Early picture of the old 7th hole (now 9th) with the 15th hole in the background

The original 10th green, now the current 12th

Caddies were paid 7d a round (6d for the caddie and 1d for the caddie master). The first monthly medal was held on July 3rd, 1909 and, as there were only twelve holes in play, a ruling was made that the members playing in competitions only had the privilege of playing the holes in rotation as they appeared on the competition cards. Under all other circumstances the twelve holes had to be played consecutively.

Hon Rupert Beckett drives the first ball on the new course at Moortown Golf Club.

Nine months after inspecting the site, the first competitive golf was being played on a twelve-hole course with a new clubhouse. After the initial excitement of forming the club and getting it off the ground, there was no lessening in the pace of development. Weekly meetings of the Committee were held as a result of which a considerable amount of voluntary work was taken on by committee members and club members alike.

The sixth hole - 'The Spinney' - was played from a tee now in the trees between the sixteenth green and the second fairway. The green was at the left side of a clump of trees now found on the right hand side of the sixteenth fairway - a feature which still traps sliced and pushed shots from the sixteenth tee. At that time the land to the left of 'The Spinney' did not belong to Moortown.

The seventh hole was the present ninth and the eighth was Gibraltar. The ninth was the old ninth which has been remodelled slightly to form the present eleventh. A key feature of all these holes was the change in green design adopted by Dr Alister MacKenzie. Most inland courses had a cutout flat pocket-handkerchief green. But at Moortown, Mackenzie adopted his Alwoodley practice and laid the larger, undulating seaside course greens. The total length of the first nine holes was 3,127 yards with a bogey of 42.

In the first year play on the course was allowed only on six days. But, after much pressure from members, play was eventually permitted after 1 pm on Sundays, too. Green fees were 2/6 a day; visitors playing with members paid 1/- a day.

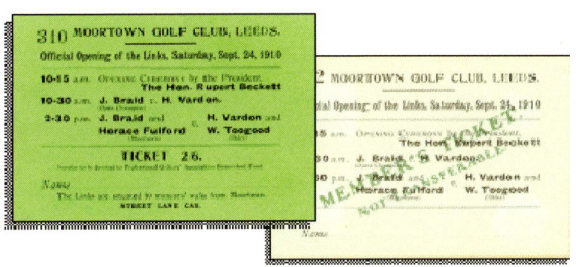

The golf course opening tickets

In 1909 and 1910 the Club negotiated the leasing of more land from neighbouring farmers to allow wider fairways and bigger greens. At this time the development and completion of the eighteen hole layout was the priority. But achieving it was not without its problems. Damage was done by hounds, cattle and geese, and farm manure was dumped regularly at the entrance to the course. There was, too, the perennial problem of trespassers. The Committee met these difficulties in consultation with the farmers, by fencing the boundaries and by engaging a constable to take the names of trespassers.

Opening of new 18 hole course by the Hon Rupert Beckett MP Sept 24th 1910

Given today's highly mechanised construction and maintenance programmes, it's hard to realise that in those days, much of the work was done by hand. Manual labour was then the order of the day but this was no problem to the Committee. In those days labour was engaged or discharged easily, and the records show that in the years up to 1914 the Committee changed the numbers and nature of the staff almost weekly. One of the hardest workers in those early years was a horse presented to the club by Henry Barran. Minutes frequently refer to its duties, and, while present committees may bemoan the taking of tough decisions, they rarely hold life and death in their hands, as the early Committee at Moortown did when, in the early 1920s, they debated the "doing away of the old horse". An animal which had done much of the heavy work in the development of the course deserved a better fate.

By Whitsuntide of 1910 the full eighteen-hole course was in play. This had been achieved by Franks and his men under the direction of Dr MacKenzie. When the course was completed the Committee arranged for two specialists in course design, H S Colt of Sunningdale and H Fowler from Walton Heath, to run the rule over it. Both expressed their approval of the course design and its construction. They were said to have been impressed at the nature of the turf and the suitability of the land's natural features as a golfing environment.

The official opening of the course was scheduled for 21st May, 1910. But it was postponed until September 24th as a mark of respect following the death of King Edward VII. James Braid and Harry Vardon were invited to play at the opening for which the club offered a prize of two guineas for the best gross score and one guinea for each of the winners, though history does not record the outcome of the event. However, it was a canny choice of players. James Braid was the reigning Open Champion when he played at Moortown having won his first Open in 1901. He went on to record further victories in 1905, 1906 and 1910. Harry Vardon's first Open win was in 1896, and he went on to win again in 1898, 1899, 1903, 1911 and 1914. In 1900 he went to America and won the U.S. Open. He remains to this day the only man to win the Open six times.

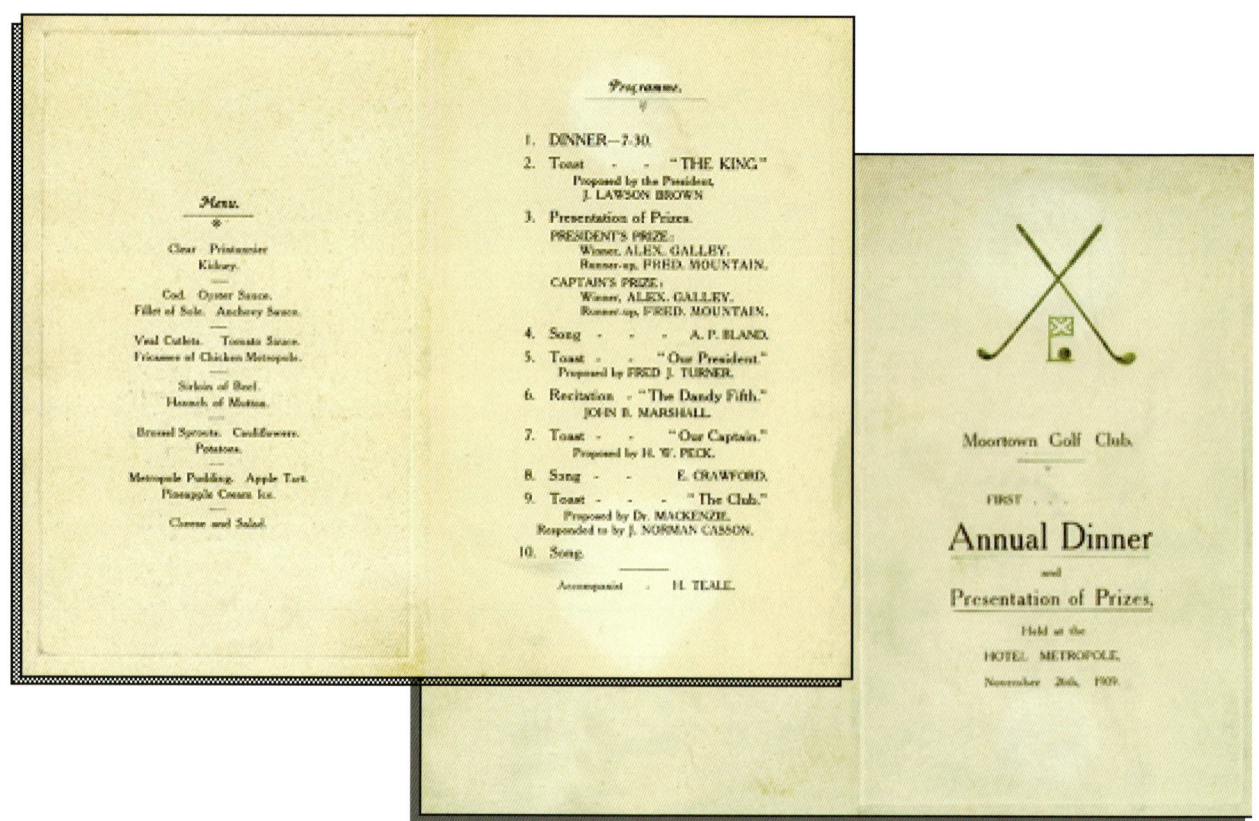

The 1st Annual Dinner & Prizegiving Dinner Menu November 1909

Both players spoke highly of Moortown's potential and a photograph taken of them at the time hung for many years in the Smoke Room as a lasting memento of one of the club's most memorable occasion.

As for the new members, by mid-1910 they were enjoying competitive golf on the new course with the men's handicap fixed from 78 with the lady's bogey score being 96 and a handicap limit of 60. Home and away matches were played with Horbury, and three major competitions - President's Prize, Captain's Prize and the Lawson-Brown Cup were inaugurated. Yet even in those very early years members posed problems to the Committee. There were those who did not pay their subscriptions on time, and in August, 1909 the Committee took a tough "name-and-shame" stance, posting the names of non-payers on the clubhouse notice board.

It is difficult to distinguish between the founders but the vision, enthusiasm and driving force of F Lawson-Brown was undoubtedly crucial. Changes in personnel are inevitable but when departures are marked by substantial dinners, then the contribution of the guests of honour must have been considerable indeed. In September, 1910, for instance, an eight-course dinner was organised at the Hotel Metropole for the Captain (F J Turner) on the occasion of his leaving Leeds. In March 1911 a dinner at the Great Northern commemorated the services of J Norman Casson as Secretary. From October of 1908 until February of 1911 Casson had been Secretary at a time when all minutes of meetings were recorded, the original membership was enrolled, new applications processed, subscriptions collected, and bills paid - all while the course and clubhouse were still under construction.

A recurring theme down the years has been the improvement of facilities. By 1911 the first course was in play and a clubhouse in use, but the Committee was not prepared to regard this as final. In 1912 a joint approach was made by Moortown and Alwoodley Golf Clubs to the Leeds City Council for the provision of electric trackless tramcars from Moortown Corner to Alwoodley. Unfortunately the request fell on stony ground and those without cars had to continue to rely on cycles or shoe leather.

Success, however, did come from the Committee's search to develop and expand the course and clubhouse. Additional plots of land adjacent to the course were leased or purchased, culminating in the purchase of an acre of land for £250 and the lease of fifteen acres close to Harrogate Road at a rent of £20 per year. The latter was an important milestone in the Club's history for it enabled the building of a new clubhouse.

A special sub-committee, chaired by Dr MacKenzie, was set up to consider course expansion and the building of a new clubhouse. The land purchased and leased near Harrogate Road was to be used for both purposes. In October 1913, plans for the new clubhouse were approved and the architect asked to obtain estimates. Building started in March, 1914 with the project financed by the issue of 6% debentures and a building society loan of £2,016 at 4½%. On April 12th, 1915, the Club moved to the new clubhouse the present building - with the entrance from Harrogate Road. In June 1915 the old clubhouse was sold for £250. Property speculators will be interested to note that in 1989 the old clubhouse was again on the market at a price of £250,000.

The Golf Course Opening Score Card

Gibraltar at Moortown. Bernard Darwin speaks of it as a hole of alarming excellence

II DR ALISTER MACKENZIE: HIS LIFE & TIMES

Dr Alister MacKenzie

It would be difficult to underestimate Dr MacKenzie's impact on international and domestic golf, even today. Three of his courses, the Augusta National, Cypress Point and Royal Melbourne are regularly named in the list of the world's top ten. And as many as a dozen MacKenzie layouts have been rated among the top one hundred in the world.

But it was here in Yorkshire where his reputation first took root, principally as a result of his work between 1907 and 1910 at the two neighbouring golf clubs of Moortown and Alwoodley. Both have holes still regarded as among the top 20 of his best-designed. They include, of course, Moortown's signature hole, the 10th, a 190-yard, par-3 which was christened 'Gibraltar' by Dr MacKenzie because its green is high on top of a rocky outcrop rising sheer from the bunkers which protect it.

Nicknamed "the Course Doctor," Alister MacKenzie was born in 1870 to Scottish parents in Normanton, Yorkshire. Like his father, he studied medicine at Cambridge University where he graduated with degrees in chemistry, medicine and natural science. A qualified doctor, MacKenzie joined his father's medical practice after Cambridge but was then called away to serve as a field surgeon in the Boer War.

There he began to study the ability of Boer soldiers to take cover in treeless fields. Ironically it was the concealed trenches of the Boers that first nurtured his design ideas for golf courses. As his military expertise in camouflage grew, he became an advisor to the Government and, during the World War I, was responsible for an official army training programme in the art of camouflage. He also helped to design trench works on the Western Front in France.

After the Boer War, MacKenzie, an avid golfer, returned to Leeds to practice medicine but subsequently abandoned his medical practice in favour of golf course architecture. His decision was in part due to his conviction that golf had very real benefits for patients, and he was quoted as saying: *"How frequently have I, with great difficulty, persuaded patients who were never off my doorstep to take up golf, and how rarely, if ever, have I seen them in my consulting rooms again!"*

Dr Alister MacKenzie portrait when Captain of the Club in 1913

His lifelong involvement with Moortown began in 1908 when, after initially designing one test hole, the legendary Gibraltar, to attract members, he was invited by the club's founders to lay out eighteen holes (with the intention of playing nine of them as soon as possible) on the land at Black Moor which had just been leased from the Lane Fox Estate. It was fortunate at the time for the founders that Dr MacKenzie happened to be in district, having almost completed the layout at Alwoodley Golf Club, which was already the talk of the golfing fraternity. He was co-opted to participate in the deliberations at Moortown and soon realised that here was golfing country par excellence.

His lasting epitaph is the course which he designed and laid out. But Dr MacKenzie became very much part of the club. He attended and often chaired many of the early meetings, was elected a Vice-President in 1909, and in 1913 he was Captain. As the Club leased more land, and as the course was further extended and the holes re-shaped, Dr MacKenzie played a continuing role and was an active Vice President for several years. However, in 1928, by which time Alister was working mostly abroad, the club turned to his younger brother, Charles, to act as a course consultant, a role in which he continued to serve untill 1933. It was then that the Green Committee decided that the need for a Consultant no longer existed as "the course has now been got more or less in its final form". Accordingly Major Charles MacKenzie was thanked in fulsome terms for his efforts for which he was awarded an honorarium and granted the coutesy of the course - a privilege he enjoyed well into the 1930s.

Meanwhile his elder brother, Alister, had become a substantial figure wherever golf was played in the English speaking world and even beyond. His international career encompassed the construction or re-modelling of more than 150 clubs throughout the world - a feat made all the more remarkable because it took place in the pre-airline days of steam railways and steam ships. In addition to the USA, Canada, Australia, New Zealand and Europe, Dr MacKenzie was also active in Argentina and Uruguay. His legacy to South America was The Jockey Club of San Isidro in Buenos Aires, Argentina and the Club de Golf del Uruguay in Montevideo. Even today each club is rated as the most exclusive in its country.

However, his early days in Yorkshire and the creation of Moortown and Alwoodley remained dear to him. Both clubs were among his favourites and he subsequently wrote that "nearly 30 years ago I made Alwoodley and Moortown, which many people consider are the best of British inland courses."

Nor did taking up residence in California dim his enthusiasm for visiting his home city. In the days of his financial plenty, he sailed the Atlantic in some style, booking the best of cabins and even shipping across his favoured American DeSoto automobile. Once back in Yorkshire it was his custom to take a luxurious suite at Harrogate's Grand Hotel overlooking the spa town's famed Gardens.

One of his last and what must have been one of his most poignant return visits to Yorkshire was to the 1929 Ryder Cup at Moortown - a tournament which was the first ever Ryder Cup on British soil, and in which Great Britain were victorious, and on one of "his" courses at that. It was and remains a course that closely conformed to Dr MacKenzie's fundamental design principles. He felt that holes should make use of the natural features of the land; that bunkering should guide the strategy for playing the course and should "frame" shots to blind greens; that contours and/or multiple tiers added interest to greens.

There are few more elevated tributes to the posterity of Dr. MacKenzie than that in the definitive book "The Life and Work of Dr. Alister MacKenzie". The authors, Tom Doak, the golf course designer, Raymund Haddock, the doctor's step grandson and Dr. James S Scott of Leeds, drew a parallel between Dr. MacKenzie and the renowned 18th century English landscape architect Capability Brown who laid out many of the nation's grandest country estates, notably Blenheim Palace. Both men, observed the authors, shared the belief that their task was to emphasise the land's existing contours and to produce dramatic water and arboreal vistas. And, in their separate ways, both left indelible landscape signatures which endure to this day. None more so in Dr MacKenzie's case than that of his most spectacular course, Cypress Point.

MacKenzie in his beloved DeSoto.
On his annual vacation to England

Dr. A. MACKENZIE
Golf Course Architect
MOOR ALLERTON LODGE LEEDS

Scale of Professional Charges and Conditions of Agreement

1—The general supervision which the Architect will give to the work is such periodical inspection by him or his deputy as may be necessary to ensure that the work is being carried out to his intentions, but constant superintendence of the work does not form part of the duties undertaken by him, and is not included for in the following scale of charges.

2—The Architect is empowered to make such deviations, alterations, additions, and omissions as he may reasonably consider desirable in the client's interests, in carrying out the work, provided that no material addition to the cost is caused thereby.

Scale of Charges

1—If the estimated cost exceeds £2,000, the percentage to be 6 per cent. plus all travelling and hotel expenses.

2—If the estimated cost does not exceed £2,000, the percentage to be 10 per cent. in the case of work costing £1,000 graduated to 6 per cent. in the case of work costing £2,000, plus travelling and hotel expenses.

3—For preliminary advice and report on the selection and suitability of a site for a Golf Course, or on the reconstruction of a Golf Course, 10 guineas and expenses a day.

4—In all cases where the material, labour, or carriage, in whole or in part, are provided by the client, the percentage of the estimated cost shall be calculated as if the work had been executed and carried out by a contractor.

NOTE—This scale of professional charges is based on the revised scale 1919 of the Royal Institute of British Architects.

The Architect's remuneration shall be payable by instalments from time to time, as the work proceeds.

Dr MacKenzie's Professional Charges

*Cypress Point Club,
Alister MacKenzie on the tee of the 16th hole.*

Dr Alister MacKenzie and Bobby Jones walking what would become Augusta National

The former United States Golf Association President, Sandy Tatum, calls Cypress Point "the Sistine Chapel of Golf". Few would argue with him. Since its opening in 1928, Cypress Point's 16th hole has been the most photogenic in the world. Initially, MacKenzie considered making the legendary 16th a do-or-die par 4, but he was persuaded otherwise by the U.S. Women's Amateur champion, Marion Hollins. "The amazing thrill of driving successfully over the ocean at the sixteenth hole at Cypress Point," he said, "more than compensates for the loss of a dozen balls."

If Cypress Point is MacKenzie's most spectacular course, there is little doubt that his best-known creation is the Augusta National in Georgia – home of the US Masters. MacKenzie was handpicked to design Augusta National by Bobby Jones, the greatest player of his generation. When Jones was upset in the first round of the 1929 U.S. Amateur at Pebble Beach, he played Cypress Point and marvelled at the layout. When they met, the pair realized their shared affection for the Old Course at St. Andrews, where Jones won the 1920 British Amateur and the 1927 British Open. In 1923, MacKenzie was hired by the Royal and Ancient Golf Club to survey the Old Course. His map hangs in the Royal and Ancient clubhouse to this day.

A wonderful partnership was formed. "MacKenzie and I managed to work as a completely sympathetic team," Jones wrote in 'Golf is My Game'. Of their work together on Augusta, he added that "of course, there was never any question that he was the architect and I his advisor and consultant." With Jones hitting test shots at his side, MacKenzie created the perfect puzzle for the masters of the game. Sadly, MacKenzie never got to see the finalised masterpiece. He died before the club opened in 1934.

During his final years, Dr MacKenzie wrote his own book, "The Spirit of St. Andrews", which included a foreword by Bobby Jones. It was never published during his lifetime. But a copy was found by his step-grandson and was published in 1995. It gave those who admire his work one last treasure from a man whose golf courses will be revered for generations to come.

Sadly, Dr MacKenzie's final days were spent in relatively straitened circumstances and in some obscurity at his home adjoining another of his courses, Pasatiempo, in Santa Cruz, California. The great Depression had taken its toll, both on new commissions, work-in-hand and the level of design fees. And his was an expensive, high-maintenance lifestyle. On New Year's Eve 1933 at a Hogmanay party at his home, he suffered a coronary thrombosis. A week later he died at home in bed. But his wish to have his ashes returned to the ancestral

Olav Arnold & Nick Leefe from Alwoodley GC with Roger Eames, Chairman of Moortown GC, at the unveiling of the Civic Trust Plaque

Civic Trust Plaque at Dr MacKenzie's Leeds house

Alister MacKenzie bronze at the Golf Hall of Fame

MacKenzie home in the Scottish Highlands turned out to be impractical. Appropriately, however, the funeral service was held in the open air close to the 6th fairway at Pasatiempo and his ashes were scattered across the course.

More permanent recognition of his life and times was unveiled in Leeds in 2005. The Civic Trust had sanctioned one of its famous circular blue plates to be installed prominently on the wall of his original home at Moor Allerton Lodge, Lidgett Lane – just a mile or so away from Moortown Golf Club whose name he had etched into the history of golf course architecture.

Worldwide recognition came in the same year when Dr Alister MacKenzie was inducted into the World Golf Hall of Fame at St Augustine, Florida, for a lifetime achievement in golf course design. Moreover his legacy continues to grow.

His definitive book, 'Golf Architecture' has become a standard text for today's budding golf course architects – not least those amateur designers who now compete annually in the Lido Prize Competition which dates back to a 1914 contest in Britain's Country Life Magazine when it was won by the then obscure designer, Alister MacKenzie. Entries were invited to design a two shot hole to challenge the best yet still offer a path for the less skilled.

Why "Lido"? Because the intention was to incorporate the best entries into the Lido golf course, being built at the time on the south shore of Long Island, New York.

Lido Golf Links, the brainchild of C.B. Macdonald and his assistant Seth Raynor, was built on property that was then marshy tideland and muddy beach. With no topographic constraints of any type, they were free to sculpt whatever shape or size hole they wished during the four-year construction of this opulent golf resort and spa. So outstanding was his complex creation, with five different routes to the green, that Macdonald and Raynor used a slightly modified version of it for the finishing hole of Lido Golf Links.

And what became of the course known then as "The Wonder at Lido"? Sadly, after a fabulously successful few years in the Roarin' 20s, the resort collapsed under the financial weight of its enormous clubhouse and construction debts when the stock market crashed. Sold off to land speculators, the club house is now a condominium complex.

But under the aegis of The MacKenzie Society, the international competition was revived in the late 1990s. In the words of the an who revived it, Bob Weisgerber, the historian at California's Green Hills Country Club, *"the express purpose is to promote the doctor's ideas and to encourage restoration consistent with his original designs and strategic thinking."*

The winning design that Dr MacKenzie submitted in the 1914 Country Life Contest

Dr Alister Mackenzie: Moortown, In His Own Words

The archival history relating to Dr MacKenzie and Moortown is, fortunately, plentiful. It would therefore be remiss of his 21st century chroniclers not to include a substantial contribution from the man himself. The following excerpts come from Dr. A MacKenzie's "Moortown and How to Play It" published in an edition of The Fairway Magazine of 1929:

"About twenty years ago, shortly after I had constructed the Alwoodley golf course, a group of prospective golfers approached me with the idea of designing a golf course on the site where the present Moortown links exists. They said they had an option of a lease from Mr. George Lane Fox. I asked them how much money was available for the purpose. They told me they could not raise more than £100 ($500). I advised them to go ahead and said that I could make at least one hole for $500 and that this would be so good that it would bring in pots of money. I constructed the eighth hole, which has since become world famous, and is known as the Gibraltar hole. This hole created such a sensation, as it was palpably so much more spectacular than anything in the district, that they had no difficulty in raising £3,000 ($15,000) to construct the remainder of the course.

As Moortown was constructed twenty years ago so it remains in all material aspects today.

Shortly after the war a new committee was appointed and they, being determined to celebrate their election by so-called improvements of the course, proceeded to fill up certain hollows and make other changes in an effort to eliminate features they considered were unfair. The members, however, found that these alterations had detracted considerably from the interest and excitement of certain holes, and they rose in their wrath and demanded that things be put back as they were before. I was again consulted and requested to comply with their demand, so Moortown was restored to its former condition.

Moortown is a heathland course. The greater part of it was originally a heather bog full of large boulders with a hard pan considerably below the surface; in other situations the peat was so thick that drainage was an extremely difficult matter. In many places we had to dig through six to eight feet of peat before we could get a hard bottom of clay to lay the drain pipes on. In other sites we were unable to get sufficient fall for drainage if we went below the peat, so we had to content ourselves with laying the drain tiles on the top of planks. Notwithstanding great efforts made to drain the course with drain tiles, this was not completely successful, so we resorted to mole drainage on the top of the tile drains. This had the desired effect and now Moortown is as dry, in spite of its heavy sub-soil of clay as most sandy heathland courses.

We had many other difficult construction jobs at Moortown. From the eighth to the fourteenth holes was a heather bog without a blade of grass, so seeding appeared to be hopeless. Fortunately there was turf in a neighbouring field. We purchased this turf and sodded between twenty and thirty acres of fairways.

Moortown is an excellent course on which to hold a competition like the Ryder Cup match, although many people would consider that it is not so suitable for medal play.

There is an enormous variety in the holes; every shot has to be placed if par figures are desired. A player is always tempted to take big risks to obtain great rewards, but on the other hand the smallest slip might lead to disaster so great that his score for even a short hole might mount to double figures."

The guide on how to master the Moortown Course

Moortown and How to Play It

By Dr. A MacKenzie
Fairway Magazine 1929

First Hole: - This was originally designed as a three-shot hole but in these days it can be and not infrequently is reached in two shots. It is essential that the green be attacked from the left. So if it is desired to reach the green in two it is necessary to place the tee shot to this side. If, on the other hand, the wind is unfavourable and it is impossible to get up in two shots, then it is essential to place the second shot left so as to have an easy approach.

Second Hole: - The green is divided into two parts; there is a large hollow on the left and a plateau on the right. The hollow part is of an artificial appearance and is somewhat freakish. It was constructed when I was ill, so that I was unable to give it an adequate amount of supervision. If the flag is placed in the hollow it is comparatively easy hole to play, but if it is placed on the plateau, as I hope it will when the Ryder Cup is played at Moortown, very accurate placing of the tee shot to the left is required so as to make it possible to get one's second near enough to the hole to have a reasonable putt for a three.

Third Hole: - In match play the hole should be cut on the left side of the green; this brings out the best features of the hole, as then it is desirable to go for the long carry on the right with one's tee shot, so as to open up the hole for one's second.

Fourth Hole: - This is the first of the one-shot holes. The shot varies according to the position of the pin.

Fifth Hole: - At this hole the flag should be placed to the right of the green. It is then advisable to go for the long carry over heather and bushes on the left so as to make the approach an easy one. Some players play an iron for safety as a long sliced shot may reach a bunker on the right.

Sixth Hole (Current 8th): - A one-shot hole. The shot varies according to the position of the tee and the flag.

Seventh Hole (Current 9th): - About 250 yards from the tee there is a stream which has been culverted in for a space of thirty yards. When the flag is placed on the right of the green, as it ought to be for match play, it is desirable to go for this gap, so as to obtain a clear run in for one's second.

Eighth Hole: (Current 10th) - Many golfers consider this the best short hole in England. It is good because the shot varies so much according to the position where the hole has been cut. When the flag is placed immediately over the bunker on the left a high lofting shot is desirable or a pitch and run with slight pulled spin. When the hole is cut on the plateau on the right then it is desirable to play the shot with a slight slice so as to hold it against the slope.

Ninth Hole: (Current 11th)- If the flag is placed on the right, it is advisable to hug the wall on the left with one's tee shot.

Tenth Hole: (Current 12th) - This hole is considerably over 500 yards and was originally designed as a three shot hole. It can be occasionally reached in two shots, but the second shot would be blind. There are, however, three tall poplars some distance behind the green and these locate the position of the green. About 300 yards from the tee there are some bunkers and heather; these can be reached by a long tee shot. A player who can drive as far as these should take an iron and play well to the left where he can hit as far as he likes.

Eleventh Hole: (Current 13th) - This is a long two-shot hole. If par figures are desired, it is desirable to go for a long tee shot on the right so as to open up the hole.

Twelfth Hole: (No longer) - This is a one-shot hole of about 180 yards. It is at its best when the hole is cut at the far right-hand corner of the green.

Thirteenth Hole: (No longer) - At this hole it is desirable to hug the wall on the left with one's tee shot. There is a hollow short of the green on the right which makes the approach shot a difficult one from this side.

Fourteenth Hole: (No longer) - A short mashie pitch.

Fifteenth Hole: - Hug the out of bounds on the left so as to obtain an easy second. This is especially important when the flag is placed in the most interesting position to the right of the green.

Sixteenth Hole: - Unless the tee shot is played over or pulled round a group of trees on the left a long drive is liable to reach a stream. The approach to the hole is distinctly easier from the left, so that it is not desirable to play short to the right with an iron.

Seventeenth Hole: (No longer) - A sliced tee shot at this hole will necessitate an extremely difficult second.

Eighteenth Hole: - It is essential to drive a long ball to the left so as to obtain an easy second shot.

1937 Aerial Shot of Moortown's 1st, 17th and 18th holes and Sandmoor's 1st, 2nd, 17th and 18th holes

III THE FIRST FIFTY YEARS

The call to arms in the Great War resulted in reduced membership and depleted income between 1914 and 1918. In order to boost membership, the club decided to accept non-playing members at a subscription of £1 for men and 10/6 for ladies, provided that they were relations of members. In order to counter the loss of income, expenditure was cut by operating a basic course maintenance programme. Additionally, volunteer members helped out with the manual labour which in those days was the norm for most green keeping operations. In the minutes is a record of thanks to the ladies for their voluntary course maintenance. Though these were dark years across Europe, hindsight reveals some of the era's lighter moments.

In 1915, for example, a Colonel Jackson was given permission for 50 men to dig trenches on the course. Many years later some of the older members suggested that the ridges on the 18th fairway indicated where these trenches had been – though the authenticity of this tale, unlike the undulations themselves, is far from clear. However, and on a more sombre note, neither the club nor its members forgot those Moortown golfers who did not return from battle and in January 1920 a roll of honour in their memory was erected in the clubhouse.

At the end of the war the process of recuperation and rehabilitation began for by 1918 the course was in a poor state. Putting it back into trim proved a formidable task, notwithstanding the valiant efforts of those who had volunteered their maintenance services during the war years.

The first priority was, of course, to make the course fit for members and visitors and to permit the staging of competitions and tournaments. By 1920 this had been achieved and in that year the club hosted the Yorkshire Amateur and Team Championships. But the key decision taken at that time was to purchase the course; from a 21st century perspective, buying seems an obvious choice. But at the beginning of the 20th century, the advantages, and the funding of it, were less clear-cut.

An option for the purchase of the course had first been granted by the landlord before World War I. But it was prudent to defer the issue during the uncertainties of the war years. However, in March 1918 there is a record of an option to buy the land for £4,000. Again, no action was taken but in December 1919 the Committee was empowered to offer £3,000. A few months later members were circularised to test their willingness and the depth of their pockets to subscribe to the purchase. The procrastination indicates the problems of financing the scheme against a post-war background of economic depression.

Eventually a sub-committee, chaired by Dr Alister MacKenzie, was set up to consider course development and it was keen to proceed with the purchase. In June 1923, Lane Fox offered a further option; this time the price was £4,150 but the option would expire in March of the following year. So it was that in December 1923 at a Special General Meeting members voted unanimously in favour of purchasing the course, and authorised the Committee to raise the necessary money. The earliest subscriptions came from those attending the meeting who stumped up £450 as an opening contribution.

The Treasurer, Norman Hurtley, drew up four schemes to raise the necessary money and, at an Extraordinary General Meeting held on March 1st 1924, the following scheme was adopted:

- each full member, including juniors, to contribute 17/6d annually for 15 years
- each lady, country, 5-day, or lady junior to contribute 13/- annually for 15 years
- members could choose to pay their subscriptions either annually or by compounding them for the entire subscription. As an inducement, those who chose the latter were able to nominate their wives/husbands or sons and daughters for election to membership.

The scheme was approved by the meeting but it did result in financial burdens. In 1927, for example, the Club owed £350 on furnishing improvements, but could only pay the interest because it was committed to repaying £500 per year for the course.

The system for managing the club's affairs has remained largely unaltered from those early years; the General Committee developed the main policies and was the key decision-making body with sub-committees set up to administer the course (Green Committee), the clubhouse (House Committee), competitions and handicaps (Golf Committee), and social activities (Billiards and Entertainment Committee, and more latterly, Social Committee).

After those momentous financial decisions taken at General Committee level and at Special and Extraordinary meetings, the more mundane workings of the sub-committees appeared trivial by comparison. But the deliberations of, for instance, the Green Committee do offer an insight into the care and attention devoted to developing and maintaining the course in first-class condition.

The committee was active in buying extra plots of land surrounding the course, and Dr MacKenzie was continually integrating this land into the layout. In its early days the Green Committee met on average six times a year; ordering materials, negotiating prices, planning work schedules, hiring and firing staff, fixing wages, and dealing with course issues were only a sample of their deliberations. Perennial problems which contemporary members will recognise included poor drainage in front of the 17th tee, cutting of the fairways containing ridges, trespassing on the course and replacing divots. One issue which no longer concerns the Committee but which caused much debate at that time was the date when winter tee-mats should be taken up.

Among the characters who were then dominant in the shaping of the Club was J F (Freddie) White, who became Chairman of the Committee in February, 1911. In April, 1911 he became honorary secretary and it was from that position that he exerted most influence. Freddie was described by his peers as having 'powers of leadership, strength of character and a dominant personality' and, as Secretary, he had wide ranging powers and responsibilities. His lasting contribution was that he was able to mould together the membership - no light task – so that Moortown Golf Club became renowned throughout Yorkshire for its hospitality and good fellowship. Freddie remained Secretary until 1933, sharing the task with J Lawson-Brown in 1930 when he was elected captain.

The current putting green was constructed in 1933 by filling in a quarry adjacent to the Professional's shop

In 1933 a quarry adjacent to the professional's shop was filled in and landscaped and the putting green built on top of it. At the same time, the starter's hut by the first tee was built, the flagstaff erected and the surrounds to the clubhouse tarmac'd. Today the hut is used for starting tournaments and for company days. But at that time strict control of the first tee and the collection of green fees was undertaken from the hut. The development was provided for the club through the generosity of T F Braime, one of Moortown's stalwarts. 'Pa' Braime as he was affectionately known, was Chairman of the General Committee from 1926 to 1944; Captain in 1934; and President from 1935 to 1954. His portrait still hangs in the entrance foyer today.

Bryon Hutchinson in front of the original starter's hut

By 1939 the course was in the form which many present day members would recognise. There had been on-going experimentation with bunker placements and shapes at some holes, but the chief concern on layout was the wish of 'Pa' Braime to move the green from the hollow at the second hole to the position where it is now located. Dr MacKenzie was still consulted before major alterations of this nature were made but it was to be some years before this change was accepted and completed.

MOORTOWN GOLF CLUB FEATURE CARD

Hole	NAME	Length Yards	FEATURE	
1	Windy Ridge	499	Guide Post	330 yds.
2	Punch Bowl	415	Stream	330 "
3	Lone Pine	450	Pine Tree	200 "
4	Spinney	183		
5	Dog Leg	380	Pine Trees	180 "
6	The Major	221	Bunker	175 "
7	The Brook	412	Brook	234 "
8	Gibraltar	150		
9	Old Club House	350	Bunker, right	170 "
		3060		
10	The Long	586	Guide Post	294 "
11	The Heather	445	Dip	200 "
12	Moor Top	170		
13	Dykeside	425	Tree on Left	240 "
14	Corner	146		
15	Paddock	390	Fence Corner	137 "
16	Holly Bush	425	Stream	290 "
17	Barker's Field	345	Ditch	145 "
18	Home	410	Whins	210 "
		3342		

Total Length 6402 yards.
Positions from which measurements are made are marked
APRIL, 1929.

Feature card for the 1st Moortown Course Planner

A feature of Moortown then which members today would not easily recognise was the absence of houses surrounding the course, and the smaller number of trees around most holes. By 1935 houses were being built adjacent to the course and decisions were made to plant more trees and bushes for protective, screening and aesthetic purposes. In addition there was the natural regeneration of birch and beam species in the rough and surrounding woodland areas.

In the inter-war years there were few debates about membership. In 1920 it was decided that membership should be curtailed because golf could "no longer be played in comfort". Committees have always had to balance the income from subscriptions against the problems of over-populating the course. But within months the decision to close the lists had been rescinded and another thirty members were elected. Members resigned as they changed jobs, and some were struck off the register for non-payment of subscriptions, though it's hard to comprehend the latter in these days of expensive golf and restricted membership opportunities, particularly when the 1920 subscriptions were:

Life Members	£52. 10.0
Full Members	£5. 5.0
5-Day Members	£4. 4.0
Country Members	£3. 3.0
Lady Members	£1. 11.6
Junior Members (boys up to 18)	£1. 1.0
Junior Members (boys 18-21)	£3. 3.0
Junior Members (girls up to 18)	£1. 1.0
Junior Members (girls 18-21)	£1. 11.6

*Entrance fees were £2.5.0d for Full Members and two guineas for Country and Lady Members.

The course was very busy on Wednesdays and Saturdays in the years leading up to 1930 when the Committee decided to restrict membership to 500 - each class of membership to stand by itself but the total was not to exceed 500. It is a revealing statistic to discover that there were between one hundred and one hundred and thirty Lady Members at that time. The main debates which stemmed from membership were centred around weekend play for ladies, the supervision of the first tee and the standing of four-ball games at weekends, the latter occasioning the opening comment signed by fifty-four member in the original Suggestion Book:

"We the undersigned respectfully suggest to the Committee that 3 and 4 ball matches be officially recognised outside the hours when competitions are being held".

Advice was sought from the R and A which ruled that this was permissible according to the Rules of Golf 1 (2). The issue of weekend play for ladies generated another prominent item in the Suggestion Book, dated 26th July, 1930:

"In view of the fact that a large number of men members can only, with any degree of certainty, play on Saturdays, perhaps it is not unreasonable, that the official time for ladies teeing off on these days should be adhered to more strictly. I also suggest ladies be debarred from the course during play for such as Captain's Prize, Lawson-Brown Cup and Greenwood Shield."

This suggestion attracted twenty-five signatories but the fact that there had been voting on the question of Sunday play for ladies as far back as 1921 shows that the issue was a continuing 'pot-boiler'. To try and ease congestion on the tee on Saturdays, members of the Committee took charge of the first tee between 1.45 pm and 2.45 pm to regulate starting and to keep order.

1937 the Moor holes seen from above Green's Nursery. The old Moor Allerton course in the background

The course viewed from the other side of Harrogate Road with Sandmoor GC and the garage in the middle ground

The '30s were a good time for Moortown and its members but as the decade drew to a close, the dark clouds of war hung over Europe once again. World War II, not unnaturally, was a time of retrenchment and survival and in its early years, Moortown's committee faced a few unusual decisions when it came to civil defence and the 'dig for victory' campaigns:

- A proposal to establish a pig farm on the course was not pursued owing to too many difficulties with the regulations
- The question of growing potatoes and cabbages on the practice ground and the grazing of sheep on the course was left open, but the Club agreed to keep in close touch with the Food Production Authority
- In 1941 it was agreed that Moortown would join the list of food and shelter centres for those made homeless by air raids on Leeds. The card room was to be used for storing rations and equipment while the Secretary had to raise a volunteer team of three men and fifteen women to staff the centre
- The Committee agreed that the local air raid wardens could hold their regular meetings at the Club for the duration of the war
- An application from the local Home Guard to use the club's tractor in the event of invasion was approved
- Free use of the club was offered to R.A.F. officers stationed at Harrogate, and to officers convalescing at Harewood House Hospital
- The clubhouse was designated a rest centre for evacuees from London and the southeast
- The ladies were given permission to use the clubhouse to make camouflage netting.

Rationing of practically every commodity from food to fuel brought significant problems. Members could not use their cars for pleasure motoring so cycling and public transport became the chief means of getting to and from the club. It speaks volumes for the tenacity of members, particularly 'spending members', that the financial position of the club was never unsatisfactory. The bar and catering revenue together with income from subscriptions covered the club's basic running costs.

Harry McMinn, the Hon Secretary in 1948, on the right with J L Kirby of the Yorkshire Union

1937 aerial shot of Green's Nursery at the back of 9th and 11th greens with the 13th fairway in the foreground

But there were inconvenient moments. Food could not be served to visitors who were also restricted to only one drink from the bar; members were restricted to one main evening meal. But, war or no war, on one occasion the committee had to discipline 'certain members who had ordered and consumed two main meals in one evening'. Moreover, members of the House Committee were accused of having priority in the consumption of food.

Even on the golf course members had the problem of acquiring golf balls which were at a premium. Old balls were recovered and re-painted in an effort to play golf. Never the less, in the spirit of 'Britain can take it', members made the most of the situation and by 1943 club membership stood at 550 in the following categories.

FULL	298
LADIES	109
JUNIOR	37
COUNTRY	4
5-DAY	1
NON-PLAYING	82
LIFE	10
ARTICLE 16	9

(64 members were serving in H.M. Forces)

That year's subscription revenue was £2,400, temporary members' fees totalled £310, the club's land and buildings were valued at £12,500 and the club made net profit of £200.

Golf was played throughout the war years, though club competitions were suspended. Many efforts to raise money for charities were made with exhibition golf (J Ballantine v W Shankland) and snooker matches (S Lee v F Davis) helping to raise many hundreds of pounds. The war years were some of the most anxious and problematic that the Moortown committee had ever endured. But, problems or not, the Committee pursued a policy of advancement and improvement and looked to the future.

In 1948, after lengthy negotiations, part of the Mount Farm land which runs alongside the back of the present ninth tee and sixteenth fairway was acquired for 4/7½d per sq yard. Part of this was sold in the 1960s for houses which now back on to the beginning of the sixteenth fairway. But in 1949 a more substantial area was bought from Green's Nurseries on the south side of the fifth hole. Many years later the wisdom of the 1949 purchase paid huge dividends – the land acquired enabled the Club to build the new sixth and seventh holes in the 1980s.

Though the war was over and though Moortown was able to pursue a policy of land acquisition, the immediate post-war years were a time of continued privation and difficulty. Labour was in perpetually short supply and weekly staff changes were commonplace. War-time restrictions continued to make it difficult to obtain adequate supplies of food, petrol, beer, spirits, coal, course machinery, dressings, and materials for repairs and printing. In 1947, for example, the whisky quota for the clubhouse was limited to two bottles per day on Wednesdays and Saturdays, three bottles on Sundays and nothing at all on Mondays, Tuesdays, Thursdays and Fridays! In more liberal times stories are legion that certain members could imbibe the entire weekly quota as their own weekly consumption. Even so, membership was full but finances were not good and subscriptions for full members were increased to ten guineas with a similar sum as the entrance fee for new members.

One important element of the financial difficulties was the decrease in catering profits which dropped from a surplus of £555 in 1948 to a loss of £500 in 1949. Many reasons were advanced for the catering crisis including the reduction in members' spending power because of the prevailing economic conditions, the appointment of a new steward and, possibly, extravagance in the kitchen.

When the Club was founded the course was completely encircled by fields with the odd farmhouse dotting the landscape. Suburbanisation had begun in the 1930s and by 1939 there were housing developments close to the course. After 1945 the pace increased with housing in the Moortown and Alwoodley areas in great demand. Adjacent as they were to Moor Allerton and Sand Moor golf courses and Heath Nurseries, Moortown's boundaries were protected. But the development of Alwoodley Park and Primley Park meant that views of housing were more common from the course. Even so, Moortown has long been a popular venue for visitors. As early as 1937, forty-seven members signed a suggestion which read:

Early Moortown fourball with their trolleys

"It is suggested that the Committee give greater consideration to the members by eliminating as much as possible the inconvenience which is frequently experienced to members due to the numerous competitions which are permitted to be played on the course by parties chiefly composed of non-members and often inexperienced golfers".

The post-war period had seen an increase in the number of such parties wanting to come to Moortown, and in the 1950s all permissions for these events had to be sanctioned by the committee. Moortown was still a golf club catering largely for its members' requirements.

At this time, members played a course where the standard scratch score was 72 compared with the old bogey score of 74, par at the second and eighteenth holes having been changed from five to four. The competitive season lasting from April to October included monthly medals together with the now well established major prizes. In 1955 the Golf Society of Great Britain was founded to promote good will amongst golfers and to help further the interests of amateur golf in all its aspects. Moortown became a participating club in 1957 and since then the Club has hosted many golf meetings organised by the Society.

Problems arose in 1952 over the proposal to increase subscriptions to keep pace with the inflationary rise in the club's costs. Objection was taken by members, some of whom had paid the levy to assist in the course purchase and who were then paying a lower subscription than recently joined members. At a succession of stormy meetings over a variety of propositions and amendments it was finally agreed to operate a flat rate subscription for the various categories of members from 1953 onwards. There were, however, casualties as a result: two vice-presidents, E Penfold and J A Sykes, resigned their positions and the auditor J L Kirby resigned from the committee.

In 1956/7 options were examined to provide and improve extra accommodation for the steward and stewardess who lived in the clubhouse where the present TV room was their main living accommodation with bedrooms upstairs. It was agreed to build a bungalow in the car park which is still on site and still used by the steward and his wife.

In 1950 a suggestion in the Book asked the committee: 'to consider the introduction of a distinguishing club tie for members of Moortown Golf Club'. The result was a tie with a green background with thin brown and white lines and a small white rosebud. The idea of brown, green and white was in recognition of the valuable services given to the Club by three members - F Lawson-Brown, Arthur Green, and Freddie White. But the design of this first tie did not appeal to many members, and in 1955/6 a sub-committee designed the narrow striped tie still incorporating the colours brown, green and white.

The first fifty years of Moortown Golf Club was celebrated in 1959 by a Jubilee Ball and the Jubilee Trophy. The Jubilee Ball, attended by 379 members, was held at the club on the 25th September, 1959. A large marquee was erected near the bungalow, with a specially-laid dance floor, settees and easy chairs, and with a covered connection to the ladies' side entrance. A six-piece band was engaged, and a buffet supper was served in the Sun Lounge and Dining Room - and all for two guineas a ticket.

Jubilee year was also marked by hosting the Yorkshire Amateur Championship with two players with longstanding Moortown associations, Alex Kyle and Sam Brough, contesting the final. To complete a memorable year the only members who joined in 1909 and who were not honorary life members of the club were so made. They were Miss Elsie Greenwood, Tom Child and Edwin Penfold.

"At the end of fifty years we should pay tribute to the stalwarts of the past who had brought the Club to its present eminence. Names coming immediately to mind are J L Brown, F Turner, Dr A MacKenzie, F White, J A Sykes, S G Hobbs, F J Brown, N Hurtley, T F Braime, E Alcock, J L Kirby, W H McMinn, R B Hopkins." (Record of the AGM, 1960).

The Jubilee Ball of December 1959
Standing: Messrs K Richardson, E Binks, J L Hutton, N G Appleyard
Seated: Mrs E Binks, Mrs J L Hutton, Mrs N G Appleyard, Mrs K Richardson

The Course prior to the changes of 1989

IV THE COURSE

THE PRE-WAR COURSE

By 1939 when the club celebrated its 30th anniversary, much had been established which would be familiar to the members of today. Then, as now, Moortown offered a challenging start: a 509-yard, bogey 5 hole with a substantial expanse of fairway. The tee was elevated in such a way that the golfers of 1939 looked down a sloping fairway flanked by a birch wood spinney on the left-hand side to which the land fell away. The turf on the fairway was springy - not least because most of the course sat on a peat bed. The second shot was played through a gap in the trees which surrounded the ditch at either side of the fairway. The average golfer would play a wood and be thankful to avoid the loose shot which would have been smartly gathered in by the surrounding gorse, heather, sand and tufty grass. The professional, however, aiming for a two putt birdie, would have been tempted to play a long/medium iron to the narrow and well-bunkered green.

A short walk over a stream, across the public footpath and through a glade of trees gave access to the second tee which looked out over a parkland vista to the west. A drive too far to the left or right would find the mixture of heather and tussocky grass which was - and is - typical of the rough at Moortown. The second hole measured 415 yards and its dominating feature was a ditch which crossed the fairway on a left to right diagonal and was sixty yards short of the green whose saucer-like shape tended to attract the ball for a two putt four.

The third was a 450-yard hole which ran alongside but in the opposite direction to the second. This hole had been aptly named as Lone Pine; a single tree stood just behind and to the right of the cross bunker. It is still there today. The drive

1939 4th Hole - the Spinney Hole with a bunker on the stream before the 4th Green

line was over the left corner of the bunker, which could be carried in normal conditions. But heather and rough grass at both sides of a narrow fairway greeted the wayward shot. Most golfers, faced with a green protected on the left by sand and gorse and on the right by a shallow bunker, opted for a wood for the second shot. Again, heather and rough grass on both sides of the narrow fairway demanded a straight line.

The fourth hole, The Spinney, was, at 183 yards, the first of the short holes. Playing the tee shot from a built-up tee among the trees by the footpath required a four or five iron to reach the well-bunkered green. The ditch had to be carried with the tee shot. But in the centre, the ditch was covered over by a large bunker, so that only the duck hook or bad slice would find the water. Broken ground, gorse and trimmed birch trees lay between the tee and the ditch. The green itself was guarded by hummocks to the left and bunkers to the right. Many were the tales of woe at this hole, with out-of-bounds over the fence at the back of the green awaiting those tempted to be too bold at the tee.

*1939 5th Hole
Taken from the tee*

Over the years the fifth hole has attracted much comment; some members were enamoured of its picturesque setting. But others disparaged it as a weak test of golfing skill. In 1939 the birch wood on the left was still relatively young and the ambitious golfer could take a more direct line to the green with a tee shot. There was, however, the extra danger of out-of-bounds over the stream which meandered through the wood. The hole was 380 yards long and dog-legged to the left. From the back tee even a low handicap golfer would find their nerve tested; a veritable wilderness of gorse, heather, bushes, a ditch and two pine trees had to be avoided before the fairway was reached. The green was long and narrow but provided a reasonably flat and true putting surface.

The sixth was a long 'one-shotter' of just over 220 yards, uphill over a bunker to an undulating green with gorse wide of it to the left. Short of the green and on the left and right was the punishing 'Moortown rough' which penalised any shot slightly under hit or off-line. The card indicated a bogey 4 but the green could be hit with a well-struck wood. A clump of trees to the left of the Manor House - a dominant part of the surrounding landscape - offered the best line. But the downward slope and the undulations of the green made it a very tricky putting surface.

From its plateau on a natural terrace, the seventh tee offered a panoramic view of a broad and inviting fairway which encouraged a robust drive to make the second shot easier. The drive was downhill, but the hole was dog-legged to the right with a length of 412 yards. Long hitters kept to the left centre of the fairway in order to open up the green for the second shot which needed to avoid a bunker that bit into the right corner of the green. Off line shots would easily find the thick grass and trees on both sides of the fairway.

The next prominent - and much-loved - feature lay in a secluded glade in a wood to the left of the eighth tee. In 1926 a 'ginger beer shop' was set up to serve drinks to weekend golfers. Two years later, the generous 'Pa' Braime provided the extra cash to fund a golf shelter on the same site, 'the chalet', as it became known. In summer at weekends drinks were dispensed from the chalet and, during the week, firms holding golf days at Moortown found it a convenient 'half-way house' (by which it is known today) for entertaining guests who, like the members, could contemplate the rigours to come at the next hole.

The eighth was the fabled 'Gibraltar', so named because its sloping, plateau green was built on the top of a rock. Gibraltar was - and is - a short hole which often featured as one of the eighteen best holes selected by contemporary golf writers. A gentle slope led up to the right of the green, but this was guarded by a yawning bunker under the steep face of the rocky plateau. The eighth was the first of the "moor holes" whose heather replaced the birch and gorse of the first seven. The ninth hole took golfers up and on to Black Moor - the original peat bog which looked so attractive to the founders. From here to the fourteenth was distinctive golfing country of windswept moorland, narrow fairways, heathery rough and clumps of small birch trees.

The ninth, 350 yards long, was a bogey 4 which took golfers to the old clubhouse, still in place behind the green. The drive was from a pulpit tee surrounded by trees with out of bounds over the wall to the left and a set of bunkers on the right to catch the sliced shot. A blind drive uphill over broken ground and gorse, with the guide post to the left of centre offered the best line while out-of-bounds over the wall in Heath's Nurseries awaited hooked or pulled second shots.

The outward nine totalled 3,060 yards with the scratch man making the turn in 37 strokes. The inward nine was a little longer at 3,342 yards and began with the longest hole in the course. Though downhill for the most part, the 586-yard tenth inhibited long drivers from 'having a go' from the tee. A patch of rough grass and two shallow bunkers split the fairway some 260 yards from the tee. It meant that only the big hitters could get there in two. However, it is a matter of record that Archie Compston, in his heyday, holed a long raking brassie shot for the only two ever recorded on this hole. Most golfers at the time were happy to drive safely over the heather, dodge the bunkers to the right and reach the foot of the hill which gave on to the green. The 445-yard eleventh was parallel with the tenth, but this time uphill. The drive was blind over the crest of the hill with heather and rough grass in front and to the left and right of the fairway. Hummocks with clinging grass and heather offered an additional hazard at the crest of the hill. Most second shots required a spoon or brassie and then a pitch to the green which sloped left to right with a large bunker guarding the green to the front left and a long meandering bunker along the back right.

1939 13th hole
The Wall Hole with the stone wall on the left which separated Moortown from Moor Allerton Golf Course

The twelfth was a deceptive short hole of 170 yards to a green set at a distinct angle to the line of play. The opening was to the left and a line of bunkers covered the right front. Over the fence behind the green was out of bounds with the golfer having to retrieve his ball from another course altogether - Moor Allerton which prior to its relocation was one of two courses then adjoining Moortown.

The thirteenth tee marked the furthermost corner of the course and offered a challenging drive which had to clear heather and rough grass, then gorse on one side of the fairway and the Moor Allerton boundary wall on the other. It was a challenging prospect but even if the drive was placed dead centre, a fearsome second shot lay in store with the same problems to the left and right of the fairway, plus a cross bunker in the centre of the fairway to catch the very long drive or the topped second. If that wasn't enough, there was a depression in the approach to the green which caused so much aggravation to so many Moortown members that it became known as the 'valley of sin'.

Behind the thirteenth green was the fourteenth tee and the last of the short holes with a length of 146 yards which appeared from the tee to offer an easy bogey 3. The tee shot was played downhill to a green surrounded on three sides by bunkers and a patch of thick grass and a stream to the rear. On the left there was more of the boundary wall with Moor Allerton while to the left of the green was a copse of young trees and rough grass.

The round ended with three bogey fours and a bogey five - none longer than 425 yards but each demanding skill and accuracy. Many golfers, noted professionals included, have had victory in sight only to come unstuck at one of these holes. The drive to the fifteenth (390 yards) had to be placed on the right centre of the fairway. A topped shot caught the ditch; a quick hook, the paddock; the overdrawn shot, the long grass; and a long left of centre drive, the cross bunkers. The second shot was played uphill to a sloping green with ditch and sand on the right and a bunker on the left. In the distance, behind the green, the imposing ivy-clad Manor House offered a line to the green from different parts of the fairway. The slope on the green made a challenge of even the shortest putt.

The sixteenth was similarly challenging: out-of-bounds in the field to the left, a copse of trees to the right, and a mighty oak guarding the direct line to the hole. If the drive was true and right of centre, the ball would finish forty yards or so from the stream. A long iron or spoon would reach the green, bunkered on the left front and right sides. The green was flat and true and suggested two putts for a bogey.

1939 7th Hole
The 7th fairway from the 7th tee

1939 9th hole - The 9th Green (now 11th) in front of the Old Clubhouse.

The seventeenth was a deceptively short bogey 4 of 345 yards. Pine trees to the right by the ditch offered a challenge to the drive as did the out of bounds to the left of the ditch which separated Moortown from Sand Moor Golf Course. Twenty yards over the public footpath on the right of the fairway was the first sand trap with another thirty yards behind. Traps to the right and out of bounds to the left gave precious little margin for error. A drive to the centre or left centre left a short second shot to the large flat green.

The eighteenth was an inviting bogey 5 of 410 yards with the clubhouse beckoning just behind the green. The ideal line over the rising fairway was slightly left, but gorse and heather attracted those too far left and, if the tee shot was too wild, even an out-of-bounds on the eighteenth hole at Sand Moor. The second shot required either a brassie or spoon to reach the large green with a deep bunker on the right front, two bunkers placed crosswise on the left and a small pot bunker at the back left. Gorse bushes at the back and right of the green offered an additional hazard.

To summarise: an inward nine of 3,342 yards with a total length of 6,402 yards and a bogey score for eighteen holes of 74. Those long-standing members who remembered the 1939 course said that if a good score couldn't be returned on the outward nine, then it was difficult to make up any shots on the inward nine. Not only was it longer, but the holes were so well designed that playing to bogey was an achievement in itself and making a birdie was an event for celebration.

But, no matter how well-established the course had become, even as the pre-war period drew to a close, one of the club's leading lights, "Pa" Braime, had initiated a debate that eventually would lead to some major course changes in the years to come.

POST WAR COURSE CHANGES

Braime's starting point for the debate was a suggestion that improvements could be made to the 2nd and 17th holes. But the eventual outcome was much more ambitious. Little changed during the war years but by the 1950s, when the post-war economic strictures began to ease, there was a period of intense activity following the recommendations of J S F Morrison, the golf course architect.

Morrison had been commissioned to take a thorough look at the course and to make recommendations on the basis of Pa Braime's suggestions as well as the other ideas which had emerged during the debate which he had initiated. As a result of Morrison's deliberations, bunkers were filled in or re-shaped, greens narrowed, ridges and hollows on greens levelled, or made less severe, and significant changes were made to certain holes. In his report which was implemented in full, Morrison recommended that the club should:

- move the 1st green 3 yards to the left, reduce its width and lift it by 6 inches
- remove the mounds on the fourth and extend the bunkers inwards
- build a new green at the 2nd hole, 30 yards beyond the existing green
- relay the 17th green and move it to the left to within 5 yards of the ditch which separated the hole from the 'old' second hole at Sand Moor

Two other developments from this era had a significant effect on the course. The 1949 drought had wrought damage to tees, fairways and greens. This prompted the committee to seek out alternative water supplies. Two experts - a water diviner and a geologist - were consulted. Their recommendation was to sink a borehole at a cost of £850. In 1952 a 200 foot deep borehole was sunk to the left of the 15th hole. Then, in 1971, the committee sanctioned the installation of an irrigation system which allowed the water supply from the borehole to be pumped to all tees and greens.

Another major improvement at the time was the enlarged practice area made possible by a land swap with Moor Allerton Golf Club. The practice area occupied the same site then that it does today. But it was much, much smaller. At that time Moor Allerton, who owned the land at the bottom of Moortown's practice area, had a problem with their golfers playing the hole adjacent to Moortown's twelfth. After lengthy negotiations, Moortown gave up some land behind the 12th but gained the land adjacent to the practice area. However, the major change from the pre-war course was the lengthening of the second hole.

In the early 1960s a plot of land adjoining the Fairway to the left of the 16th hole was sold for £15,000 and houses were subsequently built on its 2.4 acres. The Club had experienced problems with housing developments near the course for a number of years, but these were compounded in the 1960s by three developments. In 1962 development rights were sought for the entire Green's Nursery site on the left of the then 9th hole. Permission was deferred but, five years later, it was granted. In the same year planning permission for housing was also granted to Sand Moor Golf Club for their land between Alwoodley Lane and Harrogate Road adjoining Moortown's 17th and 18th holes. A year earlier Moor Allerton Golf Club successfully sought planning permission to develop their golf course for housing following their planned re-location to Wike a few miles away. The effect was to bring housing development close to Moortown's 12th, 13th and 14th holes.

The club objected formally to all the applications but its arguments did not find favour with the city fathers whose decisions profoundly affected the course. Moortown was faced with three options:

- retain the course as is with minor changes to minimise the effects of the new housing
- sell the course and move elsewhere
- sell Moortown's acres zoned for building (i.e. the 9th, 10th, 11th, 12th and 13th holes) replacing the "lost" holes on land in the woods owned by the club and on additional land to be bought from Green's Nursery

Many committee meetings followed, but neither of the last two options were ever serious contenders and they were dismissed as bordering on the sacrilegious. In 1968 the first plan to alter the course involved doing away with the 12th; playing the 13th from a slightly different tee; creating new 14th and 15th holes on land to the left of the 15th and planting extensive stands of trees to screen the course from the new housing. These proposals found a wider audience when they appeared in the Yorkshire Post on March 8th 1968. Excerpts from **"MOORTOWN LOOK TO THE FUTURE"** By **Richard Dodd** are published below.

"Moortown Golf Club, situated in a quiet residential area of North Leeds, suffered a double blow when the members learnt that housing development was to take place on part of their neighbour's course, Sand Moor, and by the recent news that houses were to be built on Moor Allerton golf course, their neighbours on the other side.

The prospect of being wedged between two housing estates was disturbing and there were fears, not only among the members, that the championship course of Moortown would lose its impressive reputation in this country and also its pleasant and peaceful surroundings.

Mr. Alan Turner, chairman of the Greens Committee, has now suggested a scheme to keep the houses out of sight and, at the same time, greatly improve the existing course. The brilliance of his scheme is in its simplicity and the whole of the work, effecting only three holes, could be carried out without interfering with the present facilities.

The short 12th hole, where a pulled tee shot can finish out of bounds on the Moor Allerton course, would be scrapped. The 13th tee would be moved so that a huge area of trees could be planted about 25 yards in depth, ensuring that the houses would not be seen.

To the left of the 15th hole, there are several acres of woodland and Mr. Turner suggests building a new green in the far corner of the course. This would increase the length of the hole by about 50 yards and make it into a left-hand dog-leg (which would become the new 14th).

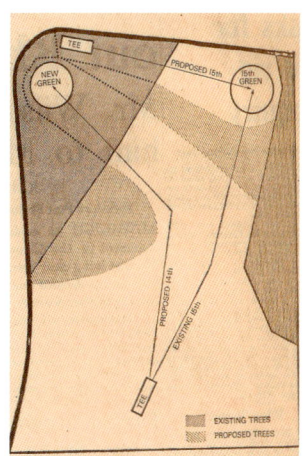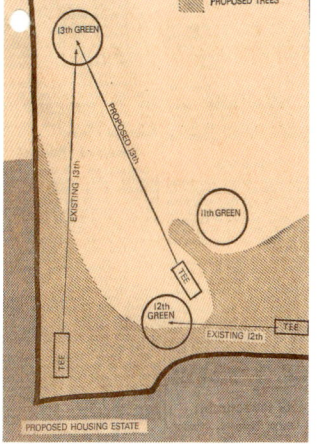

Alan Turner's suggested 14th and 15th Changes and new 13th tee in 1968

A new short hole of about 170 yards would be played from a tee near the new 14th green to the present 15th green.

If Mr Turner's idea is approved, work could be in progress without being noticed by competitors in the Brabazon Trophy, due to be played at Moortown later this year, or in club competitions. Extensive tree planting will probably begin in a few weeks time and it has been suggested that some members might like to buy groups of trees and present them to the club. Many trees may be transferred from Moortown's existing woodland.

The brilliance of the scheme notwithstanding, it did not come to fruition. Instead the Club sought either to buy parcels of land by the 9th, 14th and 17th holes, or at the least, to put restrictive covenants on their use, but legal complications and the land were to prove too costly.

In 1970 the General Committee affirmed its policy to 'stay at Moortown' and its resolve was such that even offers of over £2,000,000 for its 75 acres were turned down. But in 1972 the old third option was dusted off and given serious consideration when developers bought Green's Nursery. Moortown's plan was to sell the 12.5 acres of the moor and acquire 14.5 of scrubland zoned for public open space. Cotton Pennink, Laurie and Partners, the Club's architects, designed five new holes and the scheme looked financially viable. But negotiations with the developers were protracted and eventually they came to nothing.

However, as the new houses started to appear on the club's boundaries, so the danger of damage and injury caused by stray golf balls became more obvious, particularly at the 12th and 13th holes. The possibility of constructing a mound alongside the latter with spoil and top soil was considered, but the Club was advised by its agronomist that this would be impractical and expensive. A series of measures including additional rough, a widened fairway and the planting of mature trees were implemented instead.

At the same time there was concern about the old 2nd hole at Sand Moor which adjoined the 17th at Moortown. In the past a surprising number of members playing these holes ended up on the wrong course. But now, pulled or hooked shots from Moortown would end up amongst the houses. An extensive 'safety' strategy was proposed but was thought too radical and, as the policy was to keep the course essentially in the form designed (and hence "do-nothing" wherever possible) it was not implemented.

THE "NEW COURSE" AND THE CARRY COT EFFECT

However action became inescapable one July evening in 1984 when the vexed question of safety was thrown into sharp relief. A Moortown member had the misfortune to play a ball out of bounds at the short 12th hole. The ball shattered the windscreen of a car parked in the drive of one of the houses adjacent to the green. But inside the car on the back seat lay a baby in a carry cot. Though the carry-cot was showered with broken glass, mercifully the baby was unhurt.

Although a substantial screen of trees had grown up beside the 12th, it was clearly insufficient to prevent high balls sailing off the course and into the houses and the incident with the baby triggered off Moortown's concern for the safety of all its neighbours. Short term, the hole was shortened from 173 yards to 125 yards while longer term options were investigated.

In the early 1980s the Club's golf architects (Cotton, Pennink, Steel and Partners) were asked to report on the re-planning of the course and the practicality of using the wooded area to the left of the fifth hole. Few golfers had ever ventured into this dense woodland, and many were the sceptics who argued that those who did had nearly disappeared in the bogs. Undeterred, the Committee persisted and in 1984 the new course layout suggested by the architects was approved.

The general thrust of the report was that to obviate the problems brought about by so many houses so close to the course, the club should:
- eliminate the 12th hole
- create two new holes in the woods
- combine the 13th and 14th holes into one new hole
- consider moving the 9th green
- create a new short hole on the 17th
- re-align the 18th fairway and re-position its tee
- plant more trees on the left of the 9th fairway
- plant heather and trees to protect the 10th fairway from the 9th tee
- plant more trees between the 18th fairway and the new houses alongside it

Most of the recommendations were accepted and in 1985 work began. As with any major construction project, there were problems; the planners fretted about tree preservation orders; heavy machinery bogged down in the cleared woods; the burning of waste timber caused offence to the neighbours; grass seed failed to germinate on the new 6th and 7th holes where standing water on the fairways suggested that drainage difficulties were insurmountable. But by May 1989 and despite all the difficulties, the new course was ready for its baptism - much to the relief of the Greens Chairman, Syd Bowyer, who had undertaken the huge task - lasting almost 5 years - of arranging and overseeing the construction of the new holes.

The course was officially declared open by Sandy Sinclair, the Captain of the R&A, during the Seniors' Championship in August 1989. But it was first played a few months earlier on May 6th and the first to play it were the Captain, David Roberts, the Vice Captain, Albert Parker, the President, Alan Turner, and the Professional, Bryon Hutchinson in a gentlemen members' drawn team competition.

Since the new course came into play, considerable discussion has taken place in an effort to improve the new 14th hole and in the summer of 2000 the Club invited the US-based Tom Doak of Renaissance Golf Design Inc. to visit Moortown. Tom Doak's knowledge of Alister MacKenzie's work was formidable and he has become the architect of choice for MacKenzie Clubs worldwide. He delivered his report in August 2000 and suggested three options for the 14th: leave as is; shorten it; restore the original character of a heathland hole, encouraging heather to grow from the top of the hill to the green.

Excerpts from his report make interesting reading:
"The prevailing feeling among the membership and that of the committee, judging from the changes made over the past

*1972 13th Hole
planting of trees adjacent to the tee*

twenty years, is that Moortown has always been defined as a championship course and that no hole should be a weak link in the chain. Indeed when the committee was confronted with having to change the course because of property-line issues, the solution was to create new holes to lengthen the course from a par 69 to the modern standard of a 7000-yard, par 72 course.

What would Dr. MacKenzie say? Well he wrote an entire book on golf architecture without ever mentioning the word "par", and he harangued against routing courses simply to achieve "ideal" yardages. With this in mind I don't think MacKenzie would be satisfied with the present 14th hole.

I believe the best alternative of the fourteenth is to seek to restore the original character of the course which has been steadily disappearing over the years - namely, the open heath character of the upper holes. Originally seven holes from Gibraltar through to the 14th were on Black Moor and, of course, the original clubhouse was located there as well. It was the most appealing part of the site to the founders; the rest of the course was in a constant mode of change and expansion right through the mid-1920s. In the past ten years two of the seven holes have been sacrificed to the boundary disputes and trees have grown up between the remaining holes changing their feel significantly.

I believe that the majority of trees on the upper holes should be removed, and that the fourteenth should accentuate this objective by restoring the belt of heather on the down slope of the hill, which used to be a feature of the old par 3 14th adding a forced carry on the second shot similar to that of the current twelfth hole. The hole could be played from the present tees at 430 yards from the back and 380 or so from the whites. To allow some room for longer second shots to let off steam, I would end the heather by building one new bunker

1985 The 7th Hole construction begins

1989 The 7th Hole nearing completion

The 7th Hole today photographed after torrential rain at the 2009 Brabazon

about even with the birch tree short and right of the green, leaving about twenty yards of open approach behind it."

Some other points and conclusions suggested by Tom Doak were:

"The one other hole which I was asked specifically to comment about was the new par three 17th. It is a strong one-shotter, though it does not offer the variety and possible changes of fortune of the short par-4 hole which it replaced. As for what might be done with it, my only suggestion is that the two small bunkers on the right of the green were perhaps too similar to other holes at Moortown and particularly to those of the sixteenth green immediately before it.

Finally, my strongest argument is for removing trees on the moor, but I did notice several other areas where the course is becoming overgrown:

   a. *The left hand tee of the fourth hole is so shaded that it is impossible to maintain healthy turf and, if it is to be maintained properly, a considerable number of trees should be removed on its south and eastern sides*
   b. *The maturity of birch trees on the left of the fifth hole have closed off the possibility of cutting the corner of the dogleg, so perhaps a row of trees should be removed to allow a more reasonable left-hand line*
   c. *The trees to the left of the tees on the eighth hole make the shot from the back tee almost impossible for players who fade the ball*
   d. *The shrubbery to the right of the sixteenth hole [just across the stream] may block out a player who has hit a good drive to the right side of the fairway*
   e. *The new sixth and seventh holes are both noticeably narrower than the rest of the course, and appear out of character because of it. On most other holes the clearing is 60-75 yards and the fairway 30-45 yards; on these two it is 40 yards of clearing and 30 of fairway, which is quite severe for the average member. If possible the trees should be cut back an additional thirty feet in selected spots along the two fairways. I would even consider cutting more trees to the left of the sixth blue tee and shifting the blue and white tees another twenty yards to the left, as holding the fairway from the present line of the tee is rather awkward.*

My suggestion for the fourteenth hole is a practical one, made in the desire to further the original character of Dr. MacKenzie's design without necessitating any more costly construction on the course. The present green does not have the character of Moortown's best, but the drainage and turf conditions are much improved to the point that it is too good to tear up in the name of 'perfectionism.'

My other suggestions are made with trepidation, for I do not want to encourage tinkering with the golf course. In my humble opinion, most all of your current problems or weaknesses in the course stem from past changes to the original design by the committee or by other architects. [Indeed the 17th might not have been lost had the green not been moved alongside the boundary by J.S.F. Morrison in the 1930s.] In contrast, the holes which have been left alone continue to thrive, and that is Dr. MacKenzie's greatest legacy on four continents around the world.

My recommendation is to look back to the reasons Dr. MacKenzie and the other founders chose to build Moortown in the first place; to enjoy the beauty of the open heath and the full challenge of the game of golf and to stay true to that vision which resulted in the creation of one of England's most outstanding courses."

At the subsequent committee meeting the Chairman reported that he had discussed Tom Doak's report with the club Professional, Bryon Hutchinson, who was largely in agreement with Doak's preferred option. The feeling of the meeting was that the best way ahead lay with a mixture of his options.

In June 2000 John Nicholson Associates were commissioned to produce a Woodland Management Plan which endorsed Tom Doak's report. The committee discussed both reports, not only in relation to the 14th but also in the context of the entire course which was in danger of becoming more of a woodland than heathland course. The large increase in the number of trees had changed the texture of the grass and impaired the growth of heather. Woodland Management and the Forestry Commission were fully supportive of the suggestions for the 14th in particular and for those for the course in general. Moreover, the cost of implementing the changes would be relatively small; large grants were available from the Forestry Commission which had intimated that the scheme would have its support.

The club promptly embarked upon a substantial tree felling programme, which initially caused shocks with the members. But eventually they were won over by the obvious improvements which had resulted from the tree felling programme.

A further report received in January 2004 was to have a major impact in the first decade of the new century. The authors were Ken Moodie, a golf course architect, John Nicholson, a woodland management expert specialising in golf course work and Ken Brown, the former professional player and now a Sky television golf commentator. Their recommendations were adopted in the years that followed.

During the winter of 2004 the reconstruction and reshaping of the 3rd green and greenside bunkers was carried out under the supervision of David Sheret, the Greens Chairman and was opened in the spring of 2005.

That winter, John Wilson, the current Greens Chairman, commissioned the reconstruction to a new design of the 5th green, the greenside bunkers, the fairway bunkers and all the tees on the 4th, including the new 'mounding' to the right of the tee. They were opened in the spring of 2006.

In the winter of 2006 the new design and the rebuild of the 5th tees, the re-shaping of bunkers around the 4th green, and a new fairway bunker and new tees on the 14th were commissioned. All were opened in the spring of 2007.

Finally, in late 2007, the club agreed to the complete reconstruction of the 17th hole, with new green, greenside bunkers, a foreground bunker and new tees with heather mounds and a ditch. Simultaneously bunkers on the 14th and 15th greens were reshaped and two new fairway bunkers were constructed on the right of the 15th fairway. The work was completed by the spring of 2008.

Overleaf are photographs of each hole taken from a Helicopter Flight commissioned in 2009 for a Centenary Television production.

2006 5th hole - new greenside bunkers

2006 5th hole - new fairway bunkers

2009 The new 17th hole on the morning of the Brabazon

Clubhouse Opening on Sat 24th September with Club President Hon Rupert Beckett in the centre of the front row

V THE CLUBHOUSE

The 19th hole has a long tradition in the history of golf, nowhere more so than at Moortown where the first Committee's attention was soon directed towards the provision of such a facility. At the outset there was no clubhouse at all, but those early pioneers did have the use of a barn at Crisp's Farm (known as Moss Hall). There they could store their clubs and, at a cost of 10d, have a meal of two eggs, bread and butter, a scone and a pot of tea.

As suitable accommodation which could be converted into a clubhouse could not be found near the course, an early decision was taken to build a clubhouse with an entry from King Lane, though the committee pegged its maximum cost to £300. Where this money would come from stimulated much debate, as did the plans themselves. But eventually all the arguments were resolved amicably and the plans for the clubhouse were approved on the 15th March, 1909. Nor did members have long to wait for their new facility which was situated at the rear of the eleventh green where a block of flats now stands – the clubhouse was up and running later that year.

It provided basic facilities for changing and the storing of equipment together with a kitchen and bar. It was also used for committee meetings and rapidly became a focal point of the club. Nevertheless, continued improvements had to be made over the first few years as toilets and other amenities were added. Though highly regarded, the clubhouse had limited space and so Moortown's inaugural Annual Dinner and Prize Presentation had to be held at the Hotel Metropole in Leeds.

But with additional space an urgent requirement, the club moved in April 1915 to the new – and present - clubhouse, with an entrance off Harrogate Road and a shared drive with Sand Moor Golf Club. Now surplus to requirements, the 1909 clubhouse was sold off as a private residence. But for many years afterwards, a jug of water and glasses were left by the boundary hedge in hot weather for the benefit of golfers, perhaps because the owner was a Miss Mollie Wallace, a member and single handicap golfer!

Prior to being demolished to make way for the block of flats, the house was unoccupied for many years. But amazingly, an outdoor light was always illuminated. When a discussion at an AGM on the releasing a covenant to enable the development, one member inquired if it was possible to find out where the previous occupier had bought his light bulbs.

Over the years extensions have been made and the internal layout modified but today's clubhouse stands on the same site and with the same basic design as that of 1915. One of the alterations was to provide (at a price "not to exceed £10") an entrance from the ladies' room to a veranda which was later enclosed and enlarged to make the present mixed lounge.

Continual improvements over the years were undertaken from 1928 onwards, when alterations to the ladies' sitting room and locker room were requested. These alterations were major, expensive and required some rebuilding but the ladies contributed £300 towards the costs. In addition over 100 ladies gave 5/- (25p) each towards the furnishings. In 1931 after the decorations were completed, the ladies' committee minutes recorded "what pleasure is derived from our beautiful room".

But their ambitions did not stop there; the ladies embarked on a course of continuous improvement. In 1932 it was decided to purchase a Welsh dresser "with a limit of £15". "An elegant piece" was finally secured, but over budget, at a cost of £22.10s. Pewter and brasses were bought and a

The original new clubhouse which shared a drive with Sand Moor, 1915.

"good strong fire screen" was deemed necessary to prevent accidents to the carpet from the open fire. In 1935 the present grandfather clock was bought. Even now, there are many who say that the ladies' lounge is the most attractive room in the clubhouse, with its large bay window overlooking the 18th fairway.

In 1937 Pa Braime, who was a generous benefactor to Moortown and President of the Club at the time, suggested that a new small room, possibly for bridge, be added to the veranda next to the ladies' lounge with steps outside. The entire cost of this room, including the furnishings, chairs, carpet, curtains and card tables was met by Mr Braime.

Two years later, in early 1939 the Ladies refurbished their lounge out of their own funds. As their contribution the men's committee offered a weighing machine which was declined "as there was no particular need". They would, however, "like to have a cigarette machine". How times have changed.

In 1915 the clubhouse closing times were more restrictive than those of today – in the darker months of October to February, the clubhouse closed at 7.30 p.m. except on Wednesdays and Saturdays when it shut at 8.00 p.m. Between March and September, however, closing times were an hour later.

The income from catering and the bar was a major source of revenue and both sets of accounts were scrutinised in detail at the monthly meetings of the House Committee. Searching questions were asked and investigations conducted if the profit margins failed to meet their targets, or if there were any marked changes in income and/or expenditure. Manageresses, stewards, stewardesses came and went with a frequency which seems to be an occupational hazard of the catering and licensed trade. For a short period, contract catering was tried, but for most of the time the club preferred to employ its own staff.

Then as now, the problems facing House Committees were familiar ones: the quality of food, the attitude and availability of the staff, and the cleanliness of the premises. But in the inter-war period some unusual issues surfaced. In 1934 a reduction of one penny was made in the price of whisky, gin and rum. Those were the days when inflation was not a recognisable economic problem.

The number of staff employed in the clubhouse varied, but was more than at present as members then made more use of the club for dining. In January 1936, for example, 1,463 meals were served. Staff were entitled to meals as part of their terms of employment, and in 1937 the manageress satisfied the Committee that while the staff were well fed, there was no extravagance in this connection. The upstairs rooms were used as staff sleeping quarters, and in 1934 the House Committee was concerned about the need for more space as three girls had to sleep in one room.

There is no record of any complaints from the girls, but there were the usual complaints from members about catering standards. In 1936 the price of lunch was two shillings and three pence and afternoon tea one shilling, but there were complaints from the gentlemen at the smallness of the cakes supplied for tea. The Committee, ever keen to satisfy members, increased the size of the cakes, but exacted the usual retribution by doubling the price to two pence. The Committee took a brave decision, too, in 1935 when it banned the dancing of the Palais Glide because of the damage to the dance floor.

The external shell of the clubhouse has remained largely unaltered. Most will agree the architects produced a charming building of mellow design; a long, low structure which, with the passing the years, has blended itself into the background of the surroundings. The car park to the front of clubhouse has been enlarged and the old huts demolished, but those who witnessed the clubhouse opening in 1915 would still recognise its form.

Clubhouse with new bay windows fitted, 1937.

Moortown's Club House in the early days free from surrounding houses

Forty years on the club house still looking very much the same.

The clubhouse supplied the golfer with his drink and victuals in a congenial setting conducive to conversation of the good shots played and the bad luck experienced. The House Committee scrutinised the Bar and Catering Accounts for each month, for on a planned profit of 50% on catering and 35% on the bar, the revenue from these accounts was an important source of income. In August 1953, for example, the steward served 4,030 meals, 654 of which were consumed by the staff. The average price of the meals was 2/8½d and the average cost of providing them was 1/4½d. The gross profit for the month was £222.11. 8d.

Changes in eating habits were noticed in 1957 when the steward complained that he should only serve sandwiches when a lunch was not available. Since then, change has been wholesale. Most of the food is now consumed in the bar areas with the emphasis on sandwiches. Moreover the introduction of the breathalyser had a marked effect on the sale of alcohol.

Some internal reorganisation has taken place down the years the main effect of which was to remove the staff accommodation from the clubhouse. The inconvenience caused by using downstairs rooms for living accommodation, plus the fire hazards created by using the upstairs rooms, led to the building of the bungalow and the housing of staff outside the clubhouse.

But the lean days of World War II exacted a heavy toll on furnishings and fittings much of which needed replacing at the end of the war — in particular the lounge carpet. As money was short, the ladies started a fund and raised the then substantial sum of £210. This marked the first in a host of updates and refurbs throughout the club. Over the years a number of plans were mooted to enlarge and renovate the men's locker room with the possible addition of a changing room for visiting players. However, any radical changes seemed to founder on a combination of financial constraints, structural difficulties, and the traditionalists' wish to retain the lockers in their original state. However in 1976 the ageing shower units were replaced with more spacious modern units and an additional visitors changing area was provided.

The House Committee has always faced a thankless task trying to reconcile and meet the varying needs of members. Typical was the storm of criticism in 1958 that greeted the plans to remodel the Men's Smoke Room. At that time there was a small, but intimate and cosy 19th, mostly occupied by long standing members who had favourite places and frowned on strangers occupying them. One

Moortown's Welcoming front door

The refurbished Smoke Room, renamed as the Alister MacKenzie Room.

The Captain's Honour Board in the Alister MacKenzie Room.

The Billiard Room after refurbishing, 2008.

of the great ordeals in life for the newly fledged member was to enter the old 19th to buy a drink. Therefore the enlargement of the bar to its present size was largely welcomed - but not by the older members who felt something had been irretrievably lost. More recently, following a refurbishment, the Smoke Room was renamed as "The Alister MacKenzie Room" following the upsurge in the recognition of Moortown's dependence of the good doctor.

Over the years The Billiard Room has been well patronised, though snooker was its most popular game. From the 1970s onwards Moortown enjoyed a speedier game of "Three Reds", which was normally played as a best of three. The games generated many spectators with the odd wager and much jocularity. The annual Fur and Feather Night in December, featuring Three Reds, Dominoes, and Darts was a full house every time with a prize for all. However, the advent of the breathalyser had a profound effect on the 19th and The Billiard Room with the Fur and Feather one of the casualties. On one occasion Bryon Hutchinson, the then pro, arranged an exhibition snooker match between Willie Thorne and Kirk Stephens with Len Ganley officiating. Over 100 members paying £10 a head were crammed into the Billiard Room and enjoyed a memorable evening.

But the biggest - and most costly - changes came in 1999 when more than £100,000 was spent on two schemes. The first, enlarging the trolley store attached to the Pro Shop at a cost of £43,000, was not without controversy. At the time members were sceptical that the room could be filled. But the doubters reckoned without the growth of the motorized trolley and the new store is now bursting at the seams with many members unable to obtain a space.

The club house as it is today viewed from the 18th green.

New trolley store & clock tower completed, 1999.

Meanwhile inside the clubhouse, a £66,000 scheme was soon under way to provide extensive alterations in the Mixed Lounge. The original fixed divide between the lounge and dining room was replaced with a sliding glazed partition while the lounge itself, the television room and the dining room were fitted out with new carpets, furniture and décor. The opening up of the Mixed Lounge and dining room to form one big hospitality area was achieved just in time to take advantage of the club's Millennium celebrations and has had a profound effect on the life of the clubhouse, enabling increased numbers - up to 140 - to attend formal dinners and events in a much improved, roomier and attractive venue.

The dining room after being completely revamped.

Bryon's Testimonial Pro Celebrity Golf Day with all his friends

VI PROFESSIONALS, GREEN KEEPERS AND CLUBHOUSE STAFF

THE PROFESSIONALS

History has not bequeathed us a record of the impression made by the first three candidates who were bidding to become Moortown's inaugural professional in 1909. Suffice it to say that in September of that year Messrs Fernie, Ferguson and Skerington, having indicated interest in the post, were invited to display their talents in an exhibition game. None were appointed.

But later that month Horace Fulford of Bridlington became Moortown's first pro with Frank Bennett as his assistant. He certainly stood the test of time, staying at the club until 1925 when he left to take up an appointment in the West Indies. He was a teacher of renown, charging one shilling and sixpence an hour. In 1911 he set up a small showroom alongside the clubhouse and in the same year was formally congratulated by the Committee for breaking the course record at Leeds Golf Club with a round of 71. His assistant, Frank Bennett appears to have flourished, too - so much so that in 1913 Alister MacKenzie wrote a letter of reference so that he could apply for a professional's position.

Fulford's successor was T B Jolly who was to stay with the club until 1929. There then followed the 17-year tenure of R F (Jock) Ballantyne who arrived at Moortown just as preparations were under way for the hosting of the 1929 Ryder Cup. In his early years at Moortown, Jock played a 36 hole challenge match with the then up and coming Henry Cotton - 18 holes at Moortown and 18 at Ashridge in Hertfordshire. Jock won the match with a side stake of £50 - a substantial sum at that time. A larger than life character, he was a redoubtable golfer who regularly played in professional tournaments.

He endeared himself to many members, not least because he kept a pet monkey and brought it to work with him. The monkey's billet at Moortown was in a small back room at the Pro Shop where it was chained to a cast iron stove, though on fine summer days it was brought out to the first tee and sat in a tree to watch the golfers. How this would go down with today's members is uncertain. However, in common with

Frank and Fred Bennett outside the Pro's shop in 1910

Frank Bennett's recommendation letter sent by Dr Alister MacKenzie

Jock Ballantine's monkey

others of his species, the older he got, the more bad-tempered the monkey became. So much so that one day it bit its handler very badly – alas, with the direst of consequences. Rumour has it that his remains lie in an unmarked grave on the first hole.

In 1946 Jock Ballantyne called it a day at Moortown and subsequently went on to serve at two more distinguished Yorkshire clubs, Ganton and Pannal. Having had just 3 pros in 37 years, Moortown went on to have 4 in the next 18, the first of which was Bill Green.

In Bill Green's tenure, a little-known assistant named Dave Thomas joined him for two and a half years from 1952 to 53. Born in Wales in 1934, Dave went on to become one of Europe's leading professional golfers for two decades having played the British Open on 16 occasions, represented Great Britain and Ireland 4 times in the Ryder Cup, played the US Open twice and the US Masters on 5 occasions, to name but a few. Amongst his wins, was the Silentnight Trophy in 1965 at Moortown.

Five years after leaving Moortown, Dave Thomas founded his own design company with the object of bringing his considerable international golf experience to bear on the design of golf courses.

Over the last thirty years he has designed more than 70 courses worldwide, including throughout the UK and continental Europe, notably in Spain, Germany, Sweden, Italy and, France. He has also designed for clients in the Far East, Africa and the Americas. He is perhaps best known for The Belfry (the home of three Ryder Cups) and San Roque near Gibraltar.

Dave has clear and happy memories of his time at Moortown where he practised with Alan Turner and shared the assistant's position with Ted Large. Moortown's putting green, he said, was his favourite green of all time.

Meanwhile his former boss, Bill Green, continued as the pro at Moortown for nine years after which he was succeeded by Fred Bullock of Glasgow (1955-57), Oliver Wynne of Lowestoft (1957-61) and Ted Large of South Staffs (1961-4).

But then began the 40-year reign of one of Moortown's most enduring characters. Bryon Hutchinson was already a leading competitor in professional tournaments in Yorkshire and the North when he came to Moortown from Sitwell Park in Rotherham in 1964. Moreover he arrived already armed with practical experience of a MacKenzie design – Sitwell Park having been the first course that Dr MacKenzie had designed for a private client rather than for a committee.

No sooner had Bryon arrived than he promptly added to his previous achievements by breaking the course record at Rotherham by three strokes with a round of 66 in the Yorkshire Open Golf Championship. It was to be the first of a string of course records which succumbed to him. He took

Bill Green, Professional 1946-1955

Bryon Hutchinson saving from the sand

Southerndown in South Wales with a score of 67 in the Martini International in which he went on to finish in third place. This was followed by the notching up of a new course record, 65, at Scarcroft in the Yorkshire Post Cup to become the Yorkshire Professional champion for the third time. In the Bowmaker Pro-Am at Sunningdale, Bryon shot a four under par 66 to take a 1 stroke lead ahead of the Australian Peter Thomson and Scotland's George Will.

In 1970, at the age of 33, Bryon met Thomson again, this time at Walton Heath where he knocked the Australian out of the News of the World Matchplay championship. "It would not be unkind to say his victory was against all odds because Thomson had won the title 4 times and the Open championship 5 times," wrote one distinguished member of the golfing press at the time. By all accounts it was a gruelling occasion, which went to the 21st hole. In the same year Bryon became the Yorkshire professional golf champion for the fourth time at his home club of Moortown, and then went on to win the Yorkshire Open for a record fifth time at Fulford.

He was an illustrious figure, too, in the PGA which he joined in 1954. He was its captain in 1974 in which year he led the Britain and Ireland team against the USA at Pinehurst in the PGA cup – the mini Ryder Cup - an event and a venue in which he had been a team player in the previous year. In 2001 Bryon's record and contribution to the PGA was recognised by his peers with the gift of honorary life membership of the PGA. In 1989, to mark Bryon's 25 years at Moortown, a pro-am team event was held followed by a celebration dinner at which Bryon presented the club with a silver plate together with a decanter and glasses. The purpose of his presentation was to record in perpetuity the names of those Moortown members who have achieved a hole-in-one on their home course. The plate is engraved with their names while the glasses are used by those celebrating such achievements.

In 2000 Bryon represented Moortown for the first time in the MacKenzie Cup Competition at Royal Melbourne and continued to play in the event until his retirement.

Another landmark year in Bryon's tenure as the club's longest serving professional came in 2002 when he was granted a testimonial year prior to his retirement in February 2003, after 40 years at Moortown. The club organised a Testimonial

Bryon Hutchinson in his competitive era

Bryon Hutchinson playing the famous 16th at Cypress Point on a Mackenzie Cup Tour

Bryon Hutchinson writing in the golfing press of three of his favourite holes

Pro Celebrity Golf Day to which many of his old professional friends were invited, including Christie O'Connor Snr, Maurice Bembridge, John Garner and David Snell. The event was rounded off that evening with a commemorative dinner at which the keynote speaker, John Greenwood, looked back at some of the highlights of Bryon's time at Moortown. The testimonial year concluded in October with a Gala Dinner at the Majestic Hotel in Harrogate at which he presented the club with a silver salver to be known as the "Hutchinson Salver" to be played for annually in one of the Saturday medals. At the 2003 AGM, shortly after Bryon's retirement, the club offered him honorary membership as a reward for his long service. Bryon is still regularly to be seen on the fairways of Moortown.

He was succeeded in 2003 by the current pro, Martin Heggie from Carlisle Golf Club whose enthusiasm and pride in the history of Moortown soon became evident. Martin's family background was steeped in golf; his late father Brian Heggie having been Secretary at Lyme Regis and Truro. Martin had been attached to Hallowes in Sheffield and Lyme Regis before moving to Clevedon in 1992. There he combined the job of pro with that of secretary-manager for more than two years before moving north again to become only the third Professional since the war at Carlisle Golf Club.

Martin enjoyed the dual role at the North Somerset club and both he and the committee felt that combining the two roles was workable. *"I missed teaching and didn't have sufficient time to play,"* he said.

"It was difficult combining the jobs but I enjoyed it and don't regret taking it on. I've gained considerable experience. Provided the club has someone to look after the accounts, a pro can comfortably run the competitions and membership."

Martin's style is very much that of a modern manager with an interest in all aspects of the club's operations. One of the pillars of the club, Martin organises and scores all the club golf competitions. Since his arrival in Yorkshire, he has represented Moortown in all the MacKenzie Cup competitions and was a member of the Moortown teams which won the Crosby Beacon twice.

With his immense enthusiasm, IT skills, knowledge of golf, and his tireless effort, Martin has become the ideal figure to support any golf organiser. He was instrumental in helping Moortown to host the MacKenzie Cup in 2005 and the resounding success of the Centenary Festival was helped enormously by Martin and his family.

Martin Heggie Driving from the 1st during the Captain's Drive in

PROFESSIONALS

1909-1925	H. Fulford
1926-1929	T. B. Jolly
1930-1946	R. E. Ballantyne
1947-1955	W. H. Green
1956-1958	F. Bullock
1959-1961	O. Wynne
1962-1963	E. Large
1964-2002	B. Hutchinson
2003-	M. A. Heggie

GREENS STAFF

In November 1908, Mr Franks was persuaded to leave Alwoodley Golf Club to become Moortown's first green keeper at a wage of 10 shillings per week for the first 7 weeks and 28 shillings thereafter. With the assistance of three other men, his first task was to lay out nine holes under the direction of Dr MacKenzie. Franks was also given the privilege of selling clubs and balls and giving golf lessons. He must have been a remarkable character for in 1911 he was given permission by the Committee to visit and advise other clubs on course construction.

Franks was succeeded as Head Green keeper in 1920 by J Abbot who was to remain with the Club until 1945. In the 1920s his wage was four pounds a week. He had seven men on his staff, but as green keeping was still labour intensive, the Club employed casual labour for specific purposes. In 1931, for example, four boys over fourteen were employed to fill in divot holes on the fairways. Not that mechanisation had not penetrated the art of course maintenance. In 1926 the Club bought a Fordson tractor with a five-gang mower attached for £366. 0. 10d. The old horse which had given sterling service for so many years was now well and truly redundant. The pace of mechanisation continued to quicken and by 1932 purpose-built sheds were erected to house all the green keepers' equipment.

The immediate post-war years brought little relief to the problems which the club had faced during the war when only basic maintenance was possible. By 1944 the course was in a poor state. Abbot - who had been head green keeper since 1920 - died in 1945 and for a period the Club was without strong direction and leadership in this department.

Replacing good green keepers has always been a problem for Green Committees, and finding a suitable man to cover for a head green keeper who had served the Club for twenty five years and who had discovered all the tricks required to maintain the course in first-class order was no easy task. The Club was experiencing a shortage of income and, to cut costs, the Finance Committee in 1946 recommended a cut in green staff from nine to three men. There was much debate in the General Committee on this issue with the point forcibly made that the course was the bedrock on which Moortown was built and that while there had been increased mechanisation in green keeping practices, much of the work was still manual. The problem was exacerbated in 1949 when the country suffered a severe drought and no public water supply could be used for watering.

Complaints concerning the condition of the course multiplied and in 1950 L Lowcock was hired from Hallamshire Golf Club to take up the post of head green keeper at an annual salary of £8 per week, plus accommodation. His appointment marked the beginning of sustained year-on-year improvement and recovery. He was followed in 1960 by J Downes who in turn was succeeded in 1973 by Bill Fox.

In 2001 Mike MacClennan of Greenkeeping Management wrote: *"Bill has been nurturing Moortown man and boy for 28 years, heading a team comprising Ian Walsh his deputy who has been with the club for 32 years, Mick Hannam, Dennis Clarke and two apprentices Kevin Fox, Bill's son and Richard Hollingworth. "I'm happy here, we have our problems but the rewards are great", says Bill, "our team is very professional and I can guarantee the members of BIGGA a challenge for the Iseki finals".*

Bill oversaw the completion of the new 6th and 7th holes and during the Seniors Championship in August 1989 when the course was officially declared open by the R & A Captain Sandy Sinclair, Bill was presented with a Silver Tankard as a memento of the occasion.

His knowledge of the course was second to none and he held the job for 34 years until his retirement in 2007 when he handed over to the current head green keeper, Steven Robinson.

Steve was fortunate that his appointment as Head Greenkeeper in October 2007 coincided with a heavy investment programme to replace and increase the range of greenkeeping equipment, much of which was reaching – and in some instances had already reached – the end of its useful life.

1989 Presentation to The Head Greenkeeper Bill Fox by S Sinclair Captain of the R & A at the opening of the new course

This also enabled Steve and his team to present the course to a high level, regardless of the weather. Additionally, he was able to add detail to the shaping of the playing surfaces in order to achieve consistency throughout.

He was also keen to tackle, in particular, the consistency of the greens whose condition was vital to the club's reputation and standing. He had inherited a variety of styles with seven original greens, two from the late 80s and the rest built over the past decade, all conforming to USGA sand-based constructions. The aim was to reach the point at which more bent grass could be introduced to the greens so that they became drought tolerant and disease resistant and therefore capable of providing excellent year round playability.

Steve has established himself with distinction, and his course preparation for the championships held at Moortown and

2008 Greens Staff Left to Right:
John Osborne, Kevin Fox, Benjamin Leeming, Steven Robinson Head Greenkeeper, David Smith, Paul Anderson, Gary Anderson

Greens staff with their current greens equipment in 2008

Moortown's Caddie Master and Starter Peter Short

the Centenary Festival have deservedly attracted the highest of accolades from the game's governing bodies.

Mention should be made here, too, of the considerable contribution made down the years by Moortown's caddie master Peter Short (1999-2008). Always immaculately attired as the occasion demanded, Peter took control of the extended trolley store and members' equipment, mastered the intricacies of the new electric trolleys and acted with distinction as the official starter for all major and large corporate events.

CLUBHOUSE STAFF

A club licence was obtained when the clubhouse opened for use in May, 1910 and the first stewardess – a Miss Lemmon - was employed in the same month on a wage of fifteen shillings per week and was assisted by 'the girl Hettie Brown at twenty pounds per year wages'.

Another manageress, Miss Ballantyne, found herself the subject of a complaint in 1936, but about her dog - not about the perennial issues of the cost or quality of the catering. Members felt that the dog had too much of the run of the place when members were around. Miss Ballantyne, however, refused to have it kept on a chain. Displaying its customary tact and diplomacy, the Committee paid eleven shillings for a more suitable animal to protect the staff at night.

One recurring theme in the minutes of the Ladies' Committee was their dissatisfaction with catering. A certain Mr. Key in the 1930s caused endless trouble, and in the end there came the crunch. Miss Pollard, the formidable lady secretary at the time, was moved to write a stiff letter to the Club Committee.

Dear Mr White,
I am writing to inform you of the impertinence of Mr. Key on Sunday last to some of our members.
Three of the ladies ordered afternoon tea and toast and were told they could not have it served in the little card room but they could fetch it themselves from the dining room. This they had to do as it was the only way they could have it in that room.
I am most fearfully surprised as I had no idea Mr. Key had any choice in the matter of service, hence this protest on behalf of the ladies concerned.
Yours very sincerely,

There is no record of Mr White's reply - but nor were there any future mentions of Mr Key.

The Club used to appoint its own cleaners and Daisy held the position for many years until 1983 when she was replaced by Eugene - who came as something of a surprise as he was a Polish gentleman. Again, how times have changed. In a previous employment Eugene had been a maker of artificial hip joints, and if anyone was on the list for a replacement he would immediately produce the relevant brochures. It is recorded that the ladies gave him presents at Christmas 'for his cheerful help during the year'. Eventually, he was replaced by contract cleaners. In more recent times the club has been well served by the ever-cheerful Albert.

Golf stewards have come and gone over the years and one of the best remembered was Jack, who served the club for many years in the 70s and 80s. Jack was prepared to provide early morning nips for a regular number of players and, provided with a suitable sweetener, was always ready to stay until the early hours of the morning if a snooker or card school was in progress. Len McCann did a considerable period of service in the 90s, and his recall of everyone's favourite tipple was legendary.

Since 2004 John and Lorraine Alexander have provided catering and bar services for the club and have continued to offer the members value and convivial service. They, like all their staff, excelled at the series of consecutive events which made up the Centenary Festival. Operating over seven days from their catering marquee, John and Lorraine produced over 1500 top quality meals and oversaw the manning of the main marquee's large and exuberant bar.

John and Lorraine Alexander the current caterers and bar manager

Al Espinosa driving off the 9th Tee with Boomer, Diegel and Duncan

VII 1929 RYDER CUP

In its 100 year history, Moortown has been blessed with many memorable moments. Many, too, are the memorable figures who have graced its fairways and greens - from players of the Walter Hagen era to those of more modern times, like Seve Ballesteros. But, if just one of its accolades had to be singled out, there is little doubt that it would be staging of The Ryder Cup in 1929. It was a defining moment for the club. Nothing contributed more to its reputation as a championship course and the nature of the event itself ensured that the name of Moortown had been etched for ever into the history of golf.

It was distinguished twice over: it was the first time the Ryder Cup had been held on English soil and it was the first "home" victory for the host nation. The inaugural Ryder Cup had been held 2 years earlier at the Worcester Country Club in Massachusetts, USA. It's a matter of pride that Moortown and Worcester, the Ryder Club debutantes on both sides of the Atlantic, today enjoy a special and unique relationship. With their shared heritage of one of the last great sporting events founded on prestige rather than prize money, members of both clubs have played at each others' courses as individuals and in teams in recent years.

There are competing claims amongst golf historians about who first had the idea of the transatlantic competition. Suffice it to say that the process was set in motion in 1926 by Sam Ryder, an amateur golfer and wealthy entrepreneur who made his fortune selling penny packets of seeds. Having watched an unofficial international match between the Americans and British at Wentworth in 1926, Ryder announced that he would give £5 to each of the winning

Samuel Ryder the seed merchant

players, and lay on a party with champagne and chicken sandwiches. Soon afterwards Sam Ryder donated his famous gold cup and the official competition was born.

There is little in Moortown's written records on how the Ryder Cup was brought to the club - and what little there is, is scant. However, it is known that on December 16th, 1928 a Special Committee meeting was held at which there was only one item on the agenda: the Ryder Cup. The Committee heard from one of the club's leading lights, Kolin Robertson that "he had arranged for the Ryder Cup to be played at Moortown". A vote of thanks was passed for all his efforts and the dates were agreed: April 26th and 27th, 1929 and a Ryder Cup sub-committee was set up consisting of Robertson and Messrs, Kirby, Brown and White.

Many years later Kolin Robertson, writing in the Yorkshire Evening News in 1947, went into a little more detail on his role:

"The late Mr. Edward Platts and I had visions of housing this match at Leeds in 1928. I approached the British Professional Golfers' Association on the matter in the winter of 1928; met them in London, and asked for the match because Leeds had done so much for professional golf. Every member of their Committee agreed and the Moortown Club took up my suggestion with open arms".

*Ryder Cup Tournament Committee of 1929
Freddie White, Norman Hartley, Fred Lawson-Brown and Kolin Robertson, chairman*

US Team on the roof of the Savoy Hotel

US team en route on the Cunard liner Mauretania

The British team on the steps of the Majestic Hotel in Harrogate

At a General Committee meeting on March 8th, 1929, the minutes state starkly that "the minutes of the Sub Committee for the Ryder Cup were approved". Contemporary sources offer only one further mention of the event - in the minutes of March 1930, the Committee thanked Sand Moor GC for their co-operation in the parking of cars during the Ryder Cup.

Little has been recorded about the preparation of the course, except that it took a considerable time and was hampered by poor weather. However the green staff must have got it right. In an article in "Golf Illustrated" (May 3, 1929), E M Cockell wrote that "the course was in perfect condition and the greens beautiful, unusually for that time of the year, the course played fast and 70 was often broken by the players".

America's Ryder Cup Golf Team arrived in Plymouth on the Cunard Liner "Mauretania" and were photographed on the roof of the Savoy Hotel in London, while the English Team met up in Harrogate at the Majestic Hotel.

The match was played over two days - Friday and Saturday - the weather was cold and raw on Friday with steady rain in the afternoon. Saturday was brighter and dryer but the temperatures were those of late April. Not that the weather put off the fans eager for a taste of the new-fangled Anglo-American competition. Estimates of the spectators vary but appear to average 20,000 over the two days. Golf Illustrated's man at the match wrote: I believe Moortown was selected with an eye to the gate. From that point of view the selection was justified. I reckon the two days brought in 20,000 spectators."

"It was an extraordinarily well-ordered crowd. Saturday was better than Friday, only because 12 more ropes were used and the stewards began to remember that they had voices. Taken by and large the general management of the match was excellent," he added.

In another article, "The Myth of Machines" (May 1929), Robert H. K. Browning noted: "There were something like fifteen thousand present on the Saturday afternoon, and as the British hopes steadily rose and the American stocks fell, the excitement became intense. The crowd was a thoroughly sporting one — at least according to its lights — a little apt, perhaps, to indulge in shouts of "Keep tha' napper down in front. Ah cahn't see!" while the players were putting, and to leave newspapers and empty bottles lying about the margins of the course, but wildly and impartially enthusiastic over good play. And on the whole they had plenty to cheer for".

Nor was the creator of Moortown about to be left out of the coverage in the golfing press. In an article in Fairway Magazine (1929) Dr MacKenzie observed: "Moortown is essentially a course which is full of interesting strategical problems and on which the golfer is continually flirting with danger to obtain great rewards. The obvious route is usually the wrong route for the player who desires to obtain par figures. At most of the holes there are easy routes for the dubs who are content with fives, sixes and sevens, but hazardous routes for players who are attempting to get threes and fours".

He went on: "The British professionals think they know the strategy of Moortown. This may be the reason why it has been chosen for the Ryder Cup match. If the American team wish to beat them, it is essential that they study the subtlety of the course or they will suffer the same feat as befell Gene Sarazen on the Portland course at Troon some years ago. Sarazen devoted his time to practising on the old course at Troon and neglected the Portland course where the qualifying rounds were to be held. The Portland course has far more difficult strategic problems then the old course and although Sarazen was playing magnificent golf at the time, he had not learned how to play the Portland course and justly deserved his fate."

The original arrangement was that the match would be contested by two teams of eight, though Water Hagen, the US captain, would have preferred ten to accommodate all the players he had brought over. However, George Duncan, the home captain, opted to stick to the original plan. One of the two players who had to stand down as a result was Percy Alliss, who had been troubled with sciatica through the winter and was short of practice. Hagen, however, stood no-one down and chose to give everyone a game by bringing Ed Dudley and Johnny Golden into the foursomes in place of young Horton Smith and Al Watrous.

Duncan's decision to choose the best eight and play them throughout seemed sound; it eliminated any extra pressure to play well on the Friday in order to be picked for Saturday. Hagen's decision to give all his players an opportunity was open to question. Having eliminated Horton Smith from the foursomes, he had left out arguably the best player on the American side.

Caricatures of the American Ryder Cup Team from May 1929 Golf Illustrated

Caricatures of the Great Britain Ryder Cup Team from May 1929 Golf Illustrated

Al Espinosa putting, watched by Leo Diegel

Henry Cotton driving off on the 1st hole

Leo Diegel putting

The large crowds surrounding the play at Moortown were amazing for the time

THE RYDER CUP, ROUND-BY ROUND

Details of the matches below have been compiled exclusively from edited selections of articles written at the time, principally by E M Cockell ("Golf Illustrated", May 1929) and Robert H. K. Browning ("The Myth of the Machines, 1929").

Joe Turnesa putting, watched by Archie Compston, and Johnny Farrell

MATCH 1: FRIDAY FOURSOMES

Charles Whitcombe and Archie Compston had a ding-dong fight with the American champion, Johnny Farrell, and Turnesa. It began at the very first hole with the Americans reaching the 500-yard hole with two superb shots. The hole was at their mercy but Farrell, known as 'the demon putter' lost his touch and missed a two-foot putt for a win.

Compston lost one hole in the afternoon when he accidentally touched the opposing ball when it lay alongside his own in the same bunker. He and Whitcombe who had

Al Espinosa and Leo Diegel on the First Hole

been one down at the end of the first round, didn't get their noses in front again until the sixteenth. Compston almost finished the match with a superb shot from the edge of the green at the seventeenth. But fate's cruellest blow was reserved for the last hole where Whitcombe pushed his drive into the whins and incurred a drop under penalty. Meanwhile Turnesa hooked his second around his neck among the refreshment tents and found a clear lie between them from which Farrell pitched over one of the tents to within four yards of the hole and halved the match.

Charles Whitcombe explains his shot to Archie Compston

MATCH 2: FRIDAY FOURSOMES

The sensation of the morning was the play of Leo Diegel and Al Espinosa, who went round in 66 in spite of a 6 at the second. They had three 2s on their card and, with Duncan's putter working a little uncertainly, established an overwhelming lead of 7 holes at half-time - a lead which they held to the end and consolidated into a victory of 7 and 5.

Walter Hagen playing off the top of the bunker at the 18th

Archie Compston driving off

MATCH 3: FRIDAY FOURSOMES
Mitchell and Robson were always a little too good for Sarazen and Dudley. But for a slip by Robson on the last green, he and Mitchell would have gone in to lunch a hole to the good. Sarazen was playing well enough, but Mitchell and Robson were not to be shaken off and won at the 35th hole by 2 and 1.

Leo Diegel driving off

MATCH 4: FRIDAY FOURSOMES
The last match, featuring Ernest Whitcombe and Henry Cotton against Walter Hagen and Johnny Golden, drew a big gallery. Cotton played some beautiful golf, but Ernest Whitcombe was not at his best. Golden, known as "6% Johnny" because you could be sure of a safe return from him, was as steady as ever and Hagen supplied brilliance enough for two. Between them they pulled the match their way to win by 2 up.

So the foursomes finished with America leading by one point, having collected 2½ to Britain's 1½.

MATCH 5: SATURDAY SINGLES
Charles Whitcombe opposed the reigning American Open Champion, Johnny Farrell, in the top match. After they had both holed good putts on the first green for a half in four, Whitcombe, thanks to his long iron shot, obtained a glorious three at the second. His victory at the third gave him a strangle-hold which he never relaxed until the match had finished in his favour. Although Farrell was a beautiful swinger of a golf club, Charlie Whitcombe throughout both days played the chip shots and holed the putts with impeccable steadiness. Whitcombe won the last four holes before lunch to go 6 up before sailing home by 8 and 6.

MATCH 6: SATURDAY SINGLES
Archie Compston in the second match lost two holes very early to Sarazen, and had a long chase before he caught him at the tenth. They finished the morning round with Compston 1 up. In the afternoon Compston made the match a real "rough house." He won the first three holes, lost the next three, won the seventh, halved the eighth, won the ninth, and went on to finish the match by 6 and 4.

Walter Hagen driving fom the 9th Tee

MATCH 7: SATURDAY SINGLES
Abe Mitchell, unlucky as ever, played sound steady golf against the fireworks of Leo Diegel. He went round in 70 to find himself with a 5 hole deficiency. Diegel was round in 32 and 33 for a 65 - and this included a short putt missed at the seventh. Diegel eventually won by 9 and 8.

Henry Cotton playing out of the rough

Joe Turnesa drives off

MATCH 8: SATURDAY SINGLES

The Duncan-Hagen match took a huge gallery. The order of each team was decided independently, neither captain knowing the arrangement of the opposing side, but before the order was made up, Hagen had suggested that Duncan and he might play together. "All right!" said Duncan, "I may tell you that I am putting myself fourth in our team." Hagen put himself in the fourth place to meet him. He must have regretted his choice, for Duncan, who had played none too well in the foursomes, out-played Hagen in every department of the game. Duncan was round in 68 at lunch, to secure a 5 hole lead. In the afternoon he excelled with 31 for the outward half, and finished off with a 10 and 8 victory. It was a Captain's touch -superb.

MATCH 9: SATURDAY SINGLES

Aubrey Boomer, after a tremendous struggle, came in 2 up on Joe Turnesa at lunch. In the afternoon he held his lead up to the turn, and then went further ahead coming in, finishing off the match by 4 and 3.

Walter Hagen with Al Espinosa

MATCH 10: SATURDAY SINGLES

The veteran Fred Robson had a gruelling time of it with Horton Smith. There was nothing in it for the first eighteen holes. Horton Smith was putting badly, although he did play a wonderful putt on the last green in the morning; he was stymied, and pulled it round in almost a semi-circle. In the afternoon Robson went out to rattle the young American. He played the first seven holes as well as anyone could wish, but had made no impression and, from this point onwards, the young giant from Missouri began to hit the ball farther and farther, and Robson went down by 4 and 2.

Ed Dudley Al Espinosa and Horton Smith

MATCH 11: SATURDAY SINGLES

Ernest Whitcombe should have beaten Espinoza. He was dormy 2 up, but played an execrable approach putt at the thirty-fifth, and was bunkered at the thirty-sixth. All credit to Espinoza for a fighting finish and for halving the match.

The enormous Ryder Cup crowd vying for somewhere to view

The Ryder Cup scoreboard after the first day

MATCH 12: SATURDAY SINGLES

Last of all came Henry Cotton playing against Watrous, who was runner-up to Bobby Jones in the British Open Championship in 1926. After losing three of the first four holes, Cotton fought steadily, and by holing a chip for a 3 at the eighteenth, made matters square at lunch-time. In the afternoon he showed marked superiority and credited Britain with a 4 and 3 victory.

So, after a bad start by the British, there was a series of thrills and spills at the end of which Great Britain had won the Ryder Cup back from the USA by 7 points to 5 - a result greeted with frantic cheering from what in those days was the largest crowd ever seen at a golf tournament on this side of the border.

The Moortown member and working journalist, Kolin Robertson, who had done more than anyone else to bring the Ryder Cup to Yorkshire, had this to say in the Yorkshire Evening News: "It is now history how Great Britain gained such a wonderful victory; how more than 20,000 people witnessed the match, and how the City of Leeds and the Moortown Club became known throughout the golfing world. Just how much Leeds and Moortown in particular gained, I know not, but there can be few golf clubs in Great Britain which have benefited so much as a result of big tournaments held over their course".

Samuel Ryder presenting the cup to Britain's George Duncan

FOURSOMES			
UNITED STATES.		**GREAT BRITAIN.**	
J. Farrell and J. Turnesa (Halved)	½	C. A. Whitcombe and A. Compston	½
L. Diegel and A. Espinosa (7 and 5)	1	A. Boomer and G. Duncan	0
G. Sarazen and B. Dudley	0	A. Mitchell and F. Robson (2 and 1)	1
J. Golden and W. Hagen (2up)	1	B. R. Whitcombe and H. Cotton	0
Total	2½	**Total**	1½
SINGLES			
J. Farrell	0	C. A. Whitcombe (8 and 6)	1
G. Sarazen	0	A. Compston (6 and 4)	1
L. Diegel (9 and 8)	1	A. Mitchell	0
W. Hagen	0	G. Duncan (10 and 8)	1
J. Turnesa	0	A. Boomer (4 and 3)	1
Horton Smith (4 and 2)	1	Fred Robson	0
A. Espinosa (halved)	½	B. R. Whitcombe (halved)	½
A. Watrous	0	H. Cotton (4 and 3)	1
Total	2½	**Total**	5½
Grand Total	5	**Grand Total**	7

The Final Score Board

Sam Ryder with the English and American teams after the match

After the match a dinner was arranged for the players and officials from both teams at The Queens Hotel in Leeds. Copies of the menu are treasured items at Moortown.

As the Ryder Cup has increased in stature over the years, so it has spawned a literature bank of its own. The story of the Moortown match is related in detail in many of the references and memorabilia from the match still hang in the clubhouse. One treasured exhibit in the dining room is a gracious letter of thanks from Water Hagen together with a signed photograph of him following his installation as an honorary member of Moortown - the first overseas player to have been granted such an honour.

Recently the significance of the event in the city's history was recognised with the presentation by the Leeds Civic Trust of two of its distinguished blue plaques; one at the entrance to the drive and the other on the clubhouse wall overlooking the car park.

Even today when the Ryder Cup is held in Europe, the Club receives enquiries from television, the press, authors and the public about that match in 1929.

Signed photograph and letter from Walter Hagen

Copy of letter from Walter Hagen Esq., Detroit

20th August 1929

Mr Norman Hurtley
Moortown Golf Club
Harrogate Road
Alwoodley
Leeds

Dear Mr Hurtley

Will you kindly extend to the members of the Moortown Golf Club my appreciation of their thoughtfulness in electing me to honorary life membership of this club, where I enjoyed a number o pleasant and thrilling days as captain of the American Ryder Cup Team in the matches with the British. The membership card was undamaged and has been added to my collection of trophies which I will keep all my life an pass on to my son.

I am certain that of all the golf competitions in which I have participated over a period of fifteen years none was so well attended as the international match in Leeds last Spring. Your club is certainly to be congratulated upon the fine manner in which it handled what turned out to be a very interesting and history making event in international golf.

I hope to be able to make many more visits to old England when I may be able to take advantage of my membership in the Moortown Golf Club. I shall always remember Leeds as one of the most enthusiastic golfing communities in England where the people turn out in large numbers and are very appreciative of the efforts of the players and where there is a hospitable club whose members were kind hosts to the boys of American Ryder Cup Team of 1929

Yours sincerely,

(Signed) WALTER HAGEN

Sam Ryder with the Captains at the Ryder Cup Dinner at the Queens Hotel

Ryder Cup Dinner Menu

Ryder Cup Civic Trust plaque at Moortown's entrance

1961, Yorkshire Evening News. Legendary Australian golfer Peter Thomson

VIII PROFESSIONAL TOURNAMENTS AND CHAMPIONSHIPS

When it comes to the mounting of professional tournaments, the Ryder Cup of 1929 may have been Moortown's summit, but there are other distinguished peaks in its range of achievements. Three prestigious international championship events stand out as those that brought the world's best golfers to Moortown: The Yorkshire Evening News Professional Tournament, The Haig Whisky Tournament Players Championship and the Car Care Plan International Golf Tournament. There were top PGA events, too, in 1976 and 2008.

One figure in the club's history can claim much of the early credit. Not only did Kolin Robertson bring the Ryder Cup to Moortown almost single-handedly; he played the pivotal role in attracting and organising the long-standing Yorkshire Evening News series, many of which were staged at Moortown.

YORKSHIRE EVENING NEWS PROFESSIONAL TOURNAMENT 1923-1962

Kolin, an active Moortown member and a single-figure handicap golfer, was a Yorkshire Evening News journalist with a world-wide reputation as a golf writer. In the autumn of 1922 he was approached by his newspaper's proprietors to suggest a new professional golf tournament which would give a fillip to a game that promised rapid expansion in the years ahead. What foresight. In those days few golf enthusiasts had the opportunity to see top flight professional golf in Yorkshire, apart from the odd exhibition game or two. Kolin wanted to attract the cream of international golfers and his newspaper readily promised sufficient prize money to bring them within reach, notably the legendary Walter Hagen and Gene Sarazen who were due to be in England at the right time. After a few ups and downs, their services - and those of every English pro of note - were secured. The first game was staged in 1923 at Adel and was judged a great success. More than 5,000 spectators were privileged to see Herbert Jolly triumph over Walter Hagen in the finest victory of his career. Small wonder then that the Y.E.N. proprietors took only a few minutes to offer a thousand guineas for future tournaments in the series.

Two years later the tournament came to Moortown where it stayed for 2 years; again it was an outstanding and popular success with victories for Len Holland in 1925 and Charles Whitcombe in 1926. Arguably the climax was reached in 1929 when once again Moortown was the host club. It provided a classic final between Joe Turnesa and Herbert Jolly. Kolin Robertson described it as "one of the most stirring struggles in the annals of golf".

YEAR	WINNER	RUNNER UP
1923	H. C. JOLLY	WALTER HAGEN
1924	F. ROBSON	A. COMPSTON
1925	LEN HOLLAND	J. OCKENDEN
1926	C. A. WHITCOMBE	M. O'NEILL
1927	E. R. WHITCOMBE	H. C. JOLLY
1928	C. A. WHITCOMBE	H. C JOLLY
1929	JOE TURNESA	H. C. JOLLY
1930	H. C JOLLY	O. SANDERSON
1931	E. R. WHITCOMBE	T. BARBER
1932	B. HODSON	F. ROBSON
1933	A. J. LACEY	A. H. PADGHAM
1934	A. H. PADGHANI	S. H. BREWS
1935	H. COTTON	P. ALLISS
1936	R. BURTON	A. G. MATTHEWS
1937	A . J. LACEY	J. FALLON
1938	A PERRY	V. GREENHALGH
1939	D. REES	J. HARGREAVES
1944	S. KING	W. SHANKLAND
1945	A. COMPSTON	W. J. COX
1946	BOBBY LOCKE	D.REES/A.G.MATTHEWS

Early Winners

Henry Cotton having tee'd off the first at Moortown

Ed Dudley and Leo Diegel at the 1929 YEN Tournament

Bobby Locke (South Africa) holing his final putt on the 18th green at Moortown to win the 1946 Tournament

Walter Hagen and Fred Tagart teeing off the 1st hole at the 1929 YEN Tournament

Walter Hagen putting on the 18th at Moortown at the 1929 YEN Tournament

Joe Turnesa of the USA receives the cup for the 1929 Yorkshire Evening News Tournament

Y.E.News 1929 Winner, Joe Turnesa

He went on: "With the Ryder Cup match at Moortown in 1929, it was an easy matter to persuade most of the Americans to play in the event held that year. Hagen, Diegel, Dudley, Horton Smith and Joe Turnesa; they were all competitors and the latter won the event after beating Herbert Jolly at the 37th hole. It is said that Jolly simply threw the match away. True it is, he looked as though the game was in his pocket, but he missed a 2ft. putt on the 34th green, and, more disconcerting still, to Jolly at any rate, Joe Turnesa holed a 15 yard putt at the 37th hole for an eagle three and the match. Herbert Jolly, however, can always look back on Leeds with happy memories. He has won the trophy twice and has been a finalist five times".

So, too, could Kolin Robertson look back on some happy memories. Having organised the inaugural competition in 1923 as the chairman of the Tournament Committee, he went on to notch up an astonishing record. He continued as the Tournament Chairman, as well as being the referee of the finals, for most of the competitions that followed. Over the years the Yorkshire Evening News Tournaments were played over five Leeds Golf Courses, Adel (now Headingley), Moortown, Sand Moor, Cobble Hall and Temple Newsam. Many of those tournaments were held at Moortown and some of the club's most senior members can still remember spectating at the YENs during the post war years when Moortown alternated as host with Sand Moor and at a time when professional golfers used the competition as preparation for the Open.

One famous incident that took place during the 1949 Tournament was when Sam King removed the Bridge over the stream on the 16th to play his shot from the stream on to the green. He went on to win the tournament and thereafter the bridge became known as "King's Bridge".

After the competition the Lord Mayor of Leeds traditionally held a dinner for the competitors and organisers of the tournament at the Leeds Civic Hall, and some star studded names from all over the world attended, the attached toast list from the 1956 dinner shows the Moortown Captain Herbert Sutcliffe toasting the Lord Mayor and has been signed by Max Faulkner and Gary Player.

The Plaque on Kings Bridge on the 16th Hole

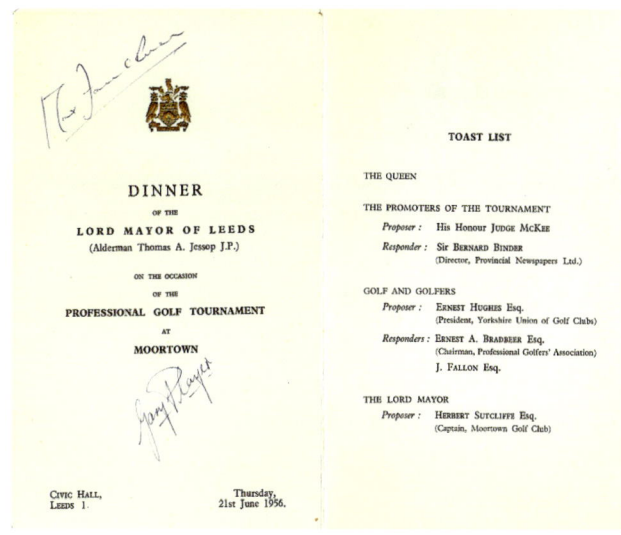

YEN 1956 Dinner menu bearing the signatures of Gary Player and Max Faulkner.

A selection of photographs from the Haig Trophy including pictures of Seve Ballesteros, Tommy Horton, Tony Jacklin, Maurice Bembridge and Brian Barnes

HAIG WHISKY TOURNAMENT PLAYERS CHAMPIONSHIP
18 Sept 1980 - 21 Sept 1980

In 1980 Moortown was invited to host the Tournament Players Championship with a breathtaking entry list of international players. No fewer than seven of them went on to become major winners: Nick Faldo, Bernard Langer, Bob Charles, Seve Ballesteros, Sandy Lyle, Greg Norman and Gary Player. Nineteen went on to represent Europe in the Ryder Cup. It also marked Moortown's entry into the age of television as the BBC broadcast live coverage of the event.

Prior to the event a pro-am competition took place and the sponsors offered two courtesy teams to the host club. The Club entered one official team and put an entry form on the notice board for interested members. The successful members were drawn and played with Jose Maria Canizares.

After two rounds, the up-and-coming Seve Ballesteros was sharing the lead with Bernard Gallacher at 5 under the par of 69. However, on the third day, Seve hit an enormous drive on eighteen. His approach shot cleared the green and landed on the putting green beyond. His reload was saved from going out of bounds from the crowd around the 18th green. It was reputed to be a wedge that landed on the putting green, but Seve's mistake meant relinquishing the lead to Bernard Gallacher who went on to win the tournament at 8 under par. Only eleven golfers ended under par.

Pos	Name	Country	To Par	R1	R2	R3	R4	Total
1	GALLACHER Bernard	SCO	-8	68	65	66	69	268
2	FALDO Nick	ENG	-5	69	68	67	67	271
2	LANGER Bernhard	GER	-5	71	64	71	65	271
4	CHARLES Bob	NZL	-3	68	67	69	69	273
4	TORRANCE Sam	SCO	-3	69	68	67	69	273
4	WATSON Denis	ZIM	-3	68	67	70	68	273
7	BALLESTEROS Seve	ESP	-2	67	66	69	72	274
7	BRITZ Tienie	RSA	-2	68	72	67	67	274
9	BARNES Brian	SCO	-1	73	67	68	67	275
9	HUMPHREYS Warren	ENG	-1	68	69	67	71	275
9	JACKLIN Tony	ENG	-1	70	67	70	68	275
12	JAMES Mark	ENG	Par	70	73	66	67	276

The Haig Trophy Results

The Haig Trophy Tournament Players' Championship draw sheet

Haig Trophy drawn Pro-am team of Peter Foreshaw, Reggie Stott, Peter Rogerson and Jose Maria Canizares

The crowd gathering at the 18th hole

THE CAR CARE PLAN INTERNATIONAL GOLF TOURNAMENT 1984 - 1986

The Car Care Plan International was part of the PGA European Tour and was organised by Moortown member Gerry Connolly in his professional capacity. It was played each year from 1982 to 1986 and was hosted by three Leeds clubs. Staged first at Moor Allerton, it moved to Sand Moor in 1983 as part of a three-year agreement. But one Saturday morning shortly after the event, which had been won by Nick Faldo, an official from Sand Moor contacted Gerry demanding that the terms of the agreement for the next 2 years be significantly revised in the club's favour. Gerry's response was to approach Moortown

Clive Clarke interviews Mark Mouland for BBC TV

Spectators surrounding the 18th green

Programme for the 1984 Car Care Plan International Tournament

The 1984 prize presentation line up with Nick Faldo, Sandy Lyle, Howard Clark, Jose Rivero, Brian Waites, Des Smyth and Ken Brown

that same Saturday morning to see if they would consider hosting the event for the following year. There was, however, a proviso - Gerry needed a decision that day so that a suitable statement could appear in the press on Monday morning.

The then Moortown Chairman, Eddie Binks, thought it would be impossible to arrange a committee meeting at such short notice but, after a series of frantic phone calls, he was able to call a meeting for 6pm that evening which was attended by every member bar one who was on holiday at the time. They were unanimous in agreeing that Moortown should accept the opportunity and so, just six hours after that morning's first telephone call, the club had secured a televised tournament for the next 3 years.

In 1984 the tournament, now hosted by Moortown and televised live, attracted all the leading professionals. A record last day crowd of crowd of 26,000 people witnessed a memorable finish by the final group including Nick Faldo, Howard Clark and Sandy Lyle and which ended with Faldo winning for the second consecutive year. His final four round score of 276 was level par and with so many of Europe's leading golfers taking part it reinforced the clubs position as one of the country's leading championship courses.

The Car Care Plan years represented the high water mark in Moortown's staging of professional tournaments in modern times. The roll of honour shows that the inaugural winner in 1982 was Brian Waites, succeeded by Nick Faldo (1983 and 1984), David J Russell (1985) and Mark Mouland (1986).

Pos	Name	Country	To Par	R1	R2	R3	R4	Total
1	FALDO Nick	ENG	0	69	70	66	71	**276**
2	CLARK Howard	ENG	1	68	68	69	72	**277**
3	RIVERO José	ESP	2	72	67	70	69	**278**
4	WAITES Brian	ENG	3	71	71	68	69	**279**
5	LYLE Sandy	SCO	4	69	72	66	73	**280**
5	SMYTH Des	IRL	4	74	69	69	68	**280**
7	BROWN Ken	SCO	5	70	71	73	67	**281**
8	DARCY Eamonn	IRL	6	69	73	70	70	**282**

Car Care Plan Pro-am team of Ian Stephenson, Paul Carrigill, Terry O'Hara and Sid Bowyer

Nick Faldo receives his trophy from Alan Longmate, Car Care's CEO

David Russell acknowledges the crowd on winning the 1985 trophy in the 1984 Car Care Plan International

Mark Mouland with the 1986 Trophy

RANK XEROX/SLAZENGER PGA CUP MATCH
October 13th to 15th 1976

The PGA Cup Matches for club professionals on both sides of the Atlantic were first played in 1973 at the Pinehurst Country Club and were structured on the format of the Ryder Cup. Moortown hosted the Cup in 1976 when the Great Britain and Ireland team was selected from the PGA Club Professional Tournament also played at Moortown. This was won by the Ilkley Professional, Bill Ferguson, but sadly Great Britain and Ireland lost 6½ to 9½.

1976 Rank Xerox Slazenger PGA Cup Match, Great Britain and Ireland team

1976 Rank Xerox Slazenger PGA Cup Match, US team

The West Berkshire golfer Paul Simpson, the winner of the 2008 Glenmuir PGA Cup

GLENMUIR PGA CLUB PROFESSIONAL CHAMPIONSHIP 2008

Qualification for the Great Britain and Ireland team was based upon performance at this event which was played at Moortown from 29th July to August 1st and whose 156-strong field included Martin Heggie, Moortown's head pro and Advanced PGA Professional.

The weather, however, was unkind. A torrential downpour on Day 1 forced play to be suspended for almost three hours with the result that 36 players had still to complete their first rounds following the lengthy rain-delay. But the weather gods had still not finished with Moortown. Further flooding and sustained rain forced the abandonment of play at 12.51pm on Day 3. With no let up in the weather and further heavy rain forecast, proceedings were called to a halt shortly after 3pm. The players resumed their third rounds at 8am on the following day, Friday, with the last group finishing at around 11.30am. A fourth round draw was then made followed by a two tee start on the 1st and tenth beginning at 1pm.

The West Berkshire golfer Paul Simpson held his nerve to defeat Andrew Barnett on the second extra hole to pick up the £10,000 first prize and near certain selection for the 2009 Great Britain and Ireland PGA Cup team.

The Glenmuir Women's PGA Professional Championship over 36 holes also took place on the final day. Tracy Loveys clinched a dramatic win after making a birdie at the 18th. The Plymouth club professional, who has twice blown leads in previous championships, drilled a five iron to 15ft and holed the putt for a 151 total to pip Gillian Stewart.

The 2008 Glenmuir PGA Cup Scoreboard

Pos	Name	Club	Country	Par	R1	R2	R3	R4	Total
1	Paul Simpson	West Berkshire	ENG	-1	73	67	67	76	283
2	Andrew Barnett	North Wales GC	WAL	-1	71	68	69	75	283
3	Paul Wesselingh	Kedleston Park GC	ENG	Par	71	70	73	70	284
4	William Barnes	RBE Golf	ENG	1	68	72	74	71	285
5	Graeme Bell	Eaglescliffe GC	ENG	2	70	69	72	75	286
5	David Shacklady	Mossock Hall GC	ENG	2	72	70	69	75	286

The PGA Cup results

John Lawson-Brown and Stewart Laws manning the on-course scoreboard at the 2008 Glenmuir PGA Cup

J J F Pennink teeing off in the 1938 English Amateur Championship

IX AMATEUR TOURNAMENTS

Moortown's unique attractions have always placed the club high on the list of courses sought out to host amateur competitions at international, national and county levels. The Boys' Championship, the Brabazon Trophy, the Seniors' Championship and the Ladies' Tournaments have all brought - and continue to bring - a distinctive and interesting group of competitors to the club. The hosting of so many prestigious amateur events is a clear sign of the esteem in which Moortown is held by The Royal & Ancient, the English Golf Union, the PGA and the Yorkshire Union. One name keeps cropping up as a Moortown winner over the years – Sir Michael Bonallack, a true amateur, a formidable player and a distinguished Secretary and Captain of the R&A.

BOYS AMATEUR CHAMPIONSHIP
(1934, 1958, 1966, 1972)

The Boys Amateur Championship, which is open to the under-18 age group, has been held at Moortown on four occasions, the first in 1934 when it was won by R.S.Burles. Moortown again hosted the event in 1958 when the winner was Russell Bradden, again in 1966 (A.A. Phillips), and finally in 1972 (G. Harvey). One outstanding player who enjoyed early success in the Boys Amateur Championship was Sir Michael Bonallack. He won in 1952, and went on to win the Amateur Championship in 1961, 1965, 1968, 1969 and 1970. Professionals who won the title earlier in their careers include Ronan Rafferty (1979), Jose Maria Olazabal (1983) and more recently, Sergio Garcia (1997).

ENGLISH AMATEUR CHAMPIONSHIP
(1938, 1962, 1980, 1994)

The English Amateur Championship was first played at Hoylake in 1925 and has an interesting format: it is played in two separate stages; the first is stroke play over two rounds of 18 holes each at two stipulated courses. The 64 lowest scores over the 36 holes then go on to compete in the match play stage which is made up of one round over 18 holes, except for the final, which is played over 36. In the inter-war years the English Amateur Championship was first hosted by Moortown in 1938 with J.J. Pennink winning 2 & 1 over the runner-up S Banks. The Championship returned to Moortown in 1962 when Sir Michael Bonallack beat M S R Lunt 2 & 1. It was back again in 1980 with P Deeble beating Peter McEvoy 4 & 3, and finally, in 1994, when M.T. Foster beat A Johnson 8 & 7.

M.T. Foster, winner of the English Amateur in 1994

J W Butler pitching out of the bunker at the 7th green in the English Amateur 1938

THE BRABAZON TROPHY
(1957, 1969, 1974, 1999, 2009)

First held in 1947, the English Men's Open Amateur Stroke Play Championship for the Brabazon Trophy was presented by Lord Brabazon of Tara and is open to all male amateur golfers, regardless of their nationality. Entrants, limited to 240 - plus those entitled to exemption - must be in possession of a handicap not exceeding ONE. The Championship consists of stroke play over 72 holes across three days. 18 holes are played on each of the first two days. After 36 of the 72 holes, the leading 40 competitors (and those tying for 40th place) play a further 36 on the third day. The winner is the competitor who returns the lowest score over the 72 holes.

The Brabazon's first of five visits to Moortown was in 1957 when the winner was Doug Sewell with a score of 287. 1969 saw a thrilling tussle between Rodney Foster and Sir Michael Bonallack with honours even on 290. In accordance with the rules, both were declared joint winners and the trophy held for six months each. The Trophy returned to Moortown in 1974 with N Sundleson being successful on a score of 291. It was back at Moortown in 1999 when the victor was Mark Side with a highly creditable 279.

THE CENTENARY BRABAZON TROPHY
15th -17th May 2009

The event's most recent appearance at Moortown – this time as part of the club's centenary - was in May when the opening

Doug Sewell celebrating his win in the 1957 Brabazon Trophy

Doug Sewell winner of the Brabazon Trophy in 1937

Mark Side receiving the Brabazon Trophy in 1999 from the Club Captain, Malcolm Tain

round was cancelled after just two hours' play on the Friday. Heavy overnight rain over Leeds, which continued throughout the morning, soon produced standing water on various parts of the course. It left officials with no alternative but to halt play at 9.05am with just 12 games on the course, and, with the forecast for the rain to continue until mid afternoon, play was abandoned at 10.30am.

Play was resumed with round two at 7am on Saturday with the tee times already allocated while the Championship was to be decided over 54 holes.

On a day of frequent showers and sunny periods following Friday's washout, Todd Adcock the English champion from Sussex fired a two-under-par 69, later matched by Hampshire's Darren Wright and Scotland's Gavin Dear, on a crowded leaderboard. But they were both overtaken by Irish international Cian Curley, who led on three-under-par 68 to set up a thrilling 36-hole final. Curley looked to be heading for a comfortable lead as he reached the turn in 31 with five of his seven birdies. But bogeys at the testing final two holes brought him back to the field.

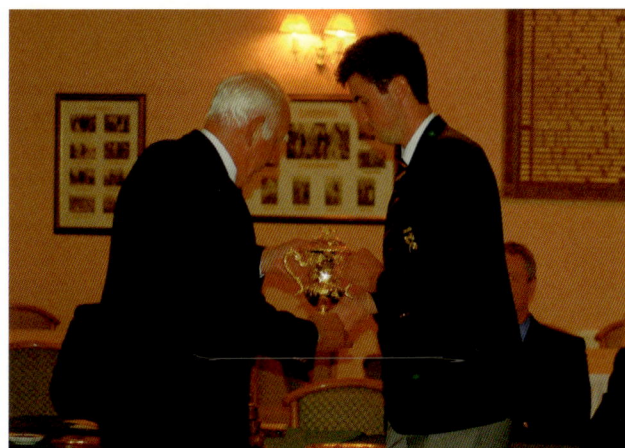

Niall Kearney receiving the 2009 Brabazon Trophy

Wright, winner of the 2009 West of England Stroke Play, also signed for 69 but he was annoyed at dropping a shot at the short 17th. Dear, a late starter, had five birdies and a double-bogey in his 69 having not felt well until the last five or six holes. Defending champion Steve Uzzell returned a three-over-par 74 and was going along smoothly at level par through 14 holes but ran up three bogeys in the last four holes.

With just one round to qualify for the final 36 holes, 59 players on 74 or better qualified for the final 36 holes.

Niall Kearney made it an Irish Sunday double when he added to his compatriot Sean Lowry's triumph in the Irish Open by winning in the teeming rain at a soggy Moortown. A closing

2009 Brabazon - The flooded course that prevented play

round of 70 for an aggregate of 208 saw the Irish international from Royal Dublin triumph by five shots from Kent champion Liam Burns who signed off with a 73.

Kearney becomes the first Irishman since Ronan Rafferty at Hunstanton in 1980 to win the Brabazon Trophy and his final round included an eagle-three on the 488-yard first when he holed his bunker shot and he added another eagle at the seventh in an outward 33. He did well to only drop two shots on the back nine as the heavens opened. He was the only player to beat par in all three rounds.

The Brabazon Cup in its full glory on the Moortown Centenary table cover

Burns, who was one of Kearney's playing partners, began two behind the Irishman but the two eagles meant he was unable to put any pressure on him. However, a 73 ended a solid week for the Kent man. In third place was 20 year old Welsh cap Joe Vickery, who had seven birdies in a closing 68 for 214, while England international Dale Whitnell climbed the leaderboard with a 69 to share fourth place with seven others on 216.

The battle for the Henriquez Salver for the best performance by a Great Britain and Ireland player aged under 20 proved a four-way tie between Tommy Fleetwood, Matt Nixon, Stiggy Hodgson and Ireland's Alan Dunbar who all finished on 216, three over par.

BOYS HOME INTERNATIONALS

Introduced at Dunbar in 1923, this competition began life as England v. Scotland but it was subsequently expanded to become a true home internationals fixture with the inclusion of representative teams from Wales and Ireland. The four home countries compete for the R&A Trophy over three consecutive days in a round robin series. The format for today's Boys Home Internationals event was established in 1996. Each fixture comprises five morning foursomes, followed by ten afternoon singles. England won the competition when it was held at Moortown in 2001.

The successful England team, winners of the 2001 Boys Home International

OTHER NOTABLE EVENTS

In 1938 the English County Championship was contested at Moortown which was won by Staffordshire; the Seniors' Open Championship was hosted in 1974 and again in 1989 with M.I. Ivor-Jones and C Green winning respectively; the 1989 English Mid-Amateur Championship was won by A. New and in 2003 the Tillman Trophy was won by J.T. Smith.

The Club also hosted the Yorkshire Amateur Championships in 1926, 1930, 1939. Moortown was also the location chosen for the Yorkshire Amateur Championship in 1951 when Ronnie Arend was the winner and in 1955 when Sam Brough won his third successive championship.

The Yorkshire Amateur Championship was again held at Moortown in 1967 (won by Rodney Foster), 1974 and 1981 (both won by Mike Kelley). In 1973 two Moortown members, Alan Booth and Howard Clark contested the final at Ganton with Howard becoming the second Moortown member to win this event. Paul Carrigill became the third Moortown winner at Alwoodley in 1978. Both Howard Clark and Paul Carrigill have since gone on to develop successful careers as professional golfers.

The 2001 Irish Boys International team

LADIES CHAMPIONSHIPS

Ladies' top level golf has been well represented at Moortown over the years. The English Ladies' Championship was won in 1955 by Mrs. R. S. Stephens. In 1978 Moortown hosted the Ladies' Home International which was won by England. Alison Nicholas went on to win the British Stroke play Championship at Moortown in 1983 before turning professional in 1984. In 2001, the ELGA County Finals were held with Yorkshire turning out the winners and in 2002 England were the victors in the English v Irish Senior Ladies.

THE DAILY TELEGRAPH INVITATION TOURNAMENT 1949

The Daily Telegraph Invitation Amateur Professional Tournament was designed primarily to broaden and enhance the experience of the leading amateurs by pairing them in foursomes matchplay with the year's most successful British, and, whenever possible, visiting American and overseas professionals.

In 1949 several members of that year's US Ryder Cup team were among the professionals competing at Moortown where members and competitors were quick to enlighten them with the course's Ryder Cup winning heritage. In addition to the Americans, the professional competitors in 1949 included Max Faulkner (Royal Mid-Surrey), Arthur Lees (Sunningdale), Dai Rees (South Herts.), Harry Weetman (Hartsbourne), Harry Bradshaw (Kilcroney) and Ken Bousfield (Coombe Hill). The amateurs included Alan Turner (Moortown), Henry Longhurst (Royal & Ancient), the famous BBC golf commentator and Alex Kyle (Sand Moor).

MOORTOWN MASTERS

The Yorkshire Order of Merit is sponsored by the Eagle Golf Centre and is a series of scratch golf competitions played throughout Yorkshire, open to all players who are members of clubs within the Yorkshire Union of Golf Clubs. The final fixture of the season to confirm the winner is the Moortown Masters played at Moortown. In 2008 Nick McCarthy finished 3rd and Nigel Sweet 5th.

The Daily Telegraph Invitation Amateur professional Foursomes programme

Leonard Crawley playing in the 1949 Daily Telegraph Amateur Professional Foursomes

Ronnie White (Royal Liverpool) playing in the 1949 Daily Telegraph Amateur Professional Foursomes

MOORTOWN JUNIOR MASTERS 1999 - 2009

Moortown set up an annual juniors' event in 1999 open to both boys and girls between 8 and 14 years of age. The event was supported by the Golf Society of Great Britain which itself holds 5 similar events around the country and is proving a breeding ground for golf stars of the future.

Mikhail Ishaq

A 12 year old from Bondhay Golf Club became the 2004 Moortown Junior Master, with a gross score of 75 playing off the yellow tees, and succeeding in winning again in 2005 and in July 2008 he fired a stunning five under par opening round of 65 in the First Point USA Scottish Boys Under-16s stroke-play championship at Glen GC in North Berwick. Mikhail fired seven birdies in a breath-taking first round. He followed this by a second round 70 to take the title by 3 shots.

Sam Connor

The runner up at Moortown in 2001 at the age of 9 and won at Little Aston in 2005. Connor, who has been handling a golf club since he could stand, joined Alsagar at the age of five and was, reportedly, described as a bit of a "boy wonder" by Ernie Els when the two met at Wentworth a couple of years later. Connor now plays off plus one and, apparently, is being eyed by England.

In 2004 the best boy was Max Williams, aged 13 from Walton Heath and the best girl was Ruth Hanson from Sand Moor. David Houlding, competing on his home course, was runner up in 2007 and the last Junior Masters winner in 2008 was Nav Dhallu.

2005 Moortown Junior Masters Competitors warming up

2004-5 Moortown Junior Masters winner Mikhail Ishaq with Moortown's Captain, Geoff Flint, Jim Wood and David Killgarriff

LAWRENCE BATLEY OVER 80s TOURNAMENT

This series of three annual tournaments held at Moortown, Leatherhead and Maxstoke Park near Birmingham gives hope to us all. Moortown was the personal choice of Lawrence Batley to host the 1992 inaugural tournament open only to the most senior of seniors. Sir Lawrence, who introduced the cash-and-carry trade to Great Britain, wanted a high quality and relatively flat course with a good golfing history and a clubhouse that could cater for around 100 players and guests. The fact that Moortown had staged major European Tour events, and had hosted PGA and Ryder Cup matches made it an ideal choice. The event provided living history, too; some of the over 80-year-old competitors had attended the Ryder Cup in 1929 and retained good, clear memories of the event and of competitors like Henry Cotton and Walter Hagen.

When Sir Lawrence first mooted the idea, there were many who were sceptical - including Bob Wilkinson who had been involved with organising seven European Tour events, the Lawrence Batley International and later The Lawrence Batley Seniors on the Seniors Tour. He explained: *"Lawrence called me into his office one day around the time of his 82nd birthday and told me he had an idea for a special golf event for golfers of over 80 years of age. He himself was still an active player and he was certain there were others like him who because of their age were still competitive but not quite good enough to win a monthly medal. He said he wanted to give these golfers an opportunity to compete on an even playing field."*

He continued: *"I thought he was mad and believed we would be lucky to muster 20 players. How wrong could I be! Well over 100 from all over the UK applied for the first event and in the end 93 teed it up. With handicaps starting as low as 5 and including five lady golfers, the first event was a huge success".*

Roger and Margaret Calvert winners of the Lawrence Batley Over 80s Tournament

The winner, Charles Mitchell of Heswall, shot 1 over his age of 80. The oldest competitor was George Nunn, 90, from Hallowes who was born 7 years before Moortown was founded and was one of those who had attended the Ryder Cup Matches in 1929. In his younger days he won the Lord Harewood trophy at Moortown in 1943 with a gross score of 76. In 2007 a unique event happened when husband and wife Roger and Margaret Calvert of Moortown won the best men and ladies awards.

The 2002 Moortown v Ilkley teams in Bryon Hutchinson's Last Match

X TEAM MATCHES

The range and quality of team matches organised for the members by the Golf Committee is fundamental to any club of standing. Moortown's members have plenty to choose from, the most prestigious being the Hudson Trophy, the Crosby Beacon and the MacKenzie Cup featured in the next chapter.

Then there are the Scratch Team competitions and the 'friendlies' with local and associated clubs that have grown with the camaraderie on the course and the conviviality of the clubhouse and finally unofficial matches, but no less durable on that account.

The 1978 Captain Arthur Clues and Bryon Hutchinson with the Hudson Trophy in 1978

THE HUDSON TROPHY
1973 – 2009
36 holes inter-club foursomes stroke play at
South Herts Golf Club

Robert A. Hudson of Portland, Oregon, was a successful businessman in the USA and a major patron of professional golf on both sides of the Atlantic. As a vice president of both the British PGA and the US PGA, he was a true exponent of the special relationship between the two countries. He was instrumental, too, in reviving the fortunes of the post-war Ryder Cup. He sponsored the American side in the 1947 contest which was held in his home state and it was there that he met Dai Rees, the professional at South Herts Golf Club, who was playing for the British Ryder Cup team.

Ten years earlier, the American Ryder Cup team had paid a visit to the South Herts club and made a pilgrimage to the local parish church in Totteridge where they placed a wreath on the grave of Harry Vardon, who had died earlier that year. When the American Ryder Cup players subsequently returned to Britain after the war, they were invited to practice at South Herts. As a result a close and lasting relationship grew up between Hudson and the Hertfordshire club which culminated in his election as an honorary life member.

His offer to sponsor a tournament at South Herts bore fruit in 1959, the year of the Club's diamond jubilee; he presented a silver casket - to be known as the Hudson Trophy - to be played for by invited clubs. After his death, the tournament was supported for a few years by the PGCA and subsequently by the PGA. But in recent years it has been run entirely by the club.

In 1973 Dai Rees invited Bryon Hutchinson, who had been captain of the PGA the previous year, to bring a Moortown team to the event. Moortown have attended frequently ever since and won the competition in 1986 and 1987 to join an illustrious list of winners including Wentworth, Sunningdale, Walton Heath and Royal Dublin, as well as the host club itself.

CROSBY BEACON
1973 – 2009, West Lancashire Golf Club

This competition takes its name from a coastal beacon adjacent to the course which acted as a navigation point for vessels entering the Mersey; the beacon no longer exists but a form of it lives on in the shape of the trophy which is said to be a good representation of the seafarers' old aid.

The competition started in West Lancashire's centenary year of 1973 and was principally limited to Lancashire clubs. But in later years Windermere and Moortown were both invited to come on board, Moortown's invitation coming from the 1980 Captain, Don Bastow, who originally hailed from Yorkshire's broad acres. The course has clearly been to Moortown's liking with wins recorded in 1984, 2000, 2003, 2006 and 2007.

The Crosby Beacon Trophy

2007 Crosby Beacon Winners: Nigel Sweet, Stephen East, Professional Martin Heggie and Andy Jones with the Vice Captain Bob Seaton holding the Trophy

YORKSHIRE 1ST DIVISION TEAM CHAMPIONSHIP

One of the region's oldest competitions, this team championship was set up in 1894 by the Yorkshire Union of Golf Clubs. It now numbers around 180 clubs in seven divisions and is competed for annually by teams of four scratch golfers playing 36 medal holes. Movement through the divisions is on the basis of promotion and demotion - six up and six down.

1979 YUGC 1st Division Team Championship: Gary Hutchinson, Paul Carrigill, Ken Baldwin Captain, Ian Stephenson and David McCarthy

Moortown hosted the Championship in 1926, 1930, 1939, 1951, 1955, 1959, 1965, 1969, 1976, 1984 and 2001, and its team has won the competition on several occasions: at Lindrick (1954), Ganton (1956), Moor Allerton (1979), Huddersfield (1981), Cleveland (1982) and Hornsea (2007).

LEEDS AND DISTRICT UNION OF GOLF CLUBS
1st DIVISION TEAM CHAMPIONSHIP

This is a 4-man team Stroke Play Scratch Event played over 36 holes. The leading eight teams from the qualifying round contest the final for the Nelson Grimshaw Trophy with the Swithenbank Trophy awarded to the player returning the lowest individual score over 36 holes.

The competition was first played in 1921 with Moortown the winners on their own course. Since then Moortown has won the Nelson Grimshaw Trophy twenty one times, most recently in 2001 and 2004 and missing out by just one shot in 2007. Stephen East won the Swithenbank Trophy in 2001 and Nigel Sweet in 2002.

Nick and Duncan McCarthy, Club Captain David Sheret, Nigel Sweet and Stephen East with the 2007 Yorkshire 1st Division Team Championship

LEEDS AND DISTRICT UNION OF GOLF CLUBS 2ND DIVISION TEAM CHAMPIONSHIP

This competition has the same format as the 1st Division Team Championship with the J. H. Robinson Trophy awarded to the winning club and the Bill Darby Trophy to the player returning the lowest individual score over 36 holes in the final. Moortown were the winners in 1947, 1994, and 1998.

LEEDS AND DISTRICT UNION OF GOLF CLUBS MONDAY NIGHT SCRATCH LEAGUE

This is a relative newcomer having started in 1966. Clubs are divided into a league of four divisions with 2-up, 2-down promotion and relegation at the end of the season. Each 3-man team plays home and away and at stake are two points for a win and 1 for a halved game. Moortown has won the 1st Division six times, most recently in 2004, 2006 and 2007.

2007 Moortown Scratch Team with their collective trophies: Nick and Duncan McCarthy, Andy Jones, Club Captain David Sheret, Stephen East, Nigel Sweet and Eddie Shoard

INTER-CLUB FRIENDLY MATCHES

The first recorded team match was in 1909 with a home-and-away fixture against Horbury Golf Club. Nowadays Moortown competes regularly against Ilkley, Moor Allerton, Ganton, Pannal, Bradford, Formby, Fulford, Lindrick and Alwoodley. All the matches are 12 a side, with the exception of Ilkley and Fulford which are 16 a side and which include the Captain and the Club Professional. At Fulford the match is played for a "Horace Fulford Wood", Horace being a former Moortown Professional. The match against Formby is played for a "Dunlop Putter", the club having being donated by John Dunlop's widow having been used by both John and his father.

An invitation from the captain to compete against Ilkley for an old Cleek golf club is one of the most highly sought after at Moortown and it's fair to say that what happens after the match is at least as memorable, if not more, than the match that precedes it. The dinners are, by tradition, well-lubricated affairs and its not unknown for the celebrants to embark on a further light-hearted game of golf, typically between the professionals "Hutchy and Hammo" v. the Rest or a cross-country Texas Scramble.

Andy Jones, Nigel Sweet Club Captain David Sheret, Stephen East and Eddie Shoard with the 2007 L and DGUC Scratch Knockout Cup

Centenary presentation made by Ian Ackroyd Captain of Bradford Golf Club to Jamie Allison after the annual match

The founders of the Castle v. Moortown Match Peter Rogerson and Jack Freeney with the Castle captain

Past Captains Fenwick Allison, Don Hanley, Malcolm Tain, Peter Rogerson and Vince Green with the Menwith Hill Captain at the dinner.

Moortown Captain David Roberts with Bryon Hutchinson, Dennis Spooner, Alan Day and Castle members Jack Freeney and Harry Davidson

The 1995 Moortown and Menwith Hills teams before their biennial match

UNOFFICIAL FRIENDLY MATCHES

Typically for a club as sociable as Moortown, many unofficial games have taken place down the years. Sometimes arranged by an individual member, sometimes by the club pro, teams have travelled to golf clubs far and wide - including The Royal Bangkok Sports Club, Dun Laoghaire and Castle Golf Club in Ireland and even a local version of the Ryder Cup against the US personnel based at Menwith Hill.

Perhaps two deserve a special mention. It was a chance meeting at Marbella in the 70s that brought Moortown's Peter Rogerson together with Jack Freeny from the Castle Golf Club in Dublin. Subsequently Jack brought over his golf pro, David Kinsella, for a golf exhibition in Birmingham and a round at Moortown with Peter and Bryon Hutchinson. Bryon subsequently took a Moortown team to play "The Castle" in Dublin where the hospitality was on a grand scale. Honour demanded that such lavish treatment had to be repaid in full. A return fixture was quickly arranged for Leeds and a further monumental celebration took place. Suffice it to say that two such events a year could be deemed injurious to the participants' health and so for the next 25 years there was one fixture a year at alternating venues where the teams competed for a "shillelagh" which was put up by Castle. Many Moortown members, including more than 10 captains, have fond memories of these events, or at least as much of them as they were able to remember.

Finally, Moortown has a special relationship of its own with the US, or in this case, that country's outpost at the Menwith Hill base near Harrogate. In the 90s a fixture was arranged with the exiles' Menwith Golf Society to stage a Yorkshire Ryder Cup at Moortown to coincide with the final day of the Ryder Cup proper. Golf was followed by dinner and, when the contest was staged in the US, the chance to see the conclusion of the real thing on television. Under the guidance of Peter Hart, Moortown took on a suitably transatlantic look with the Stars and Stripes flying, appropriate table decorations and Ryder Cup memento gifts all round. This event still takes place bi-annually.

The Moortown team assembling in the bar before their Ryder Cup encounter with Menwith Hill

Menwith Hil Match players watching the real Ryder Cup on TV

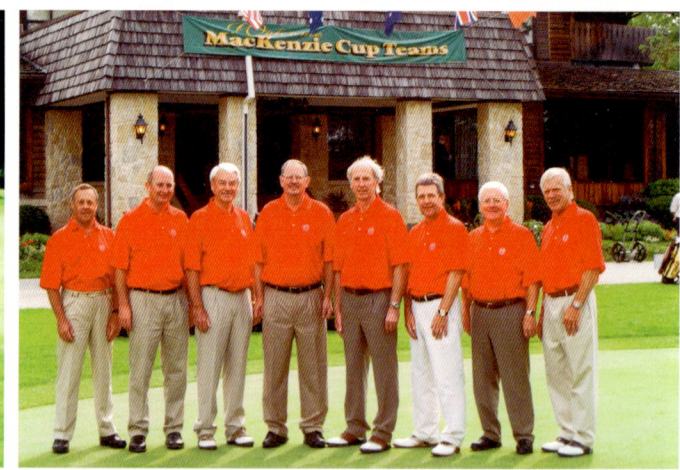

XI THE MACKENZIE CUP

HOW IT ALL BEGAN

A little over 20 years ago, four Californian golf clubs met to see how best they could mark a shared heritage.

The clubs, whose courses were all designed by the Yorkshire-born international architect, Dr. Alister MacKenzie, were Pasatiempo in Santa Cruz, near San Jose, the Meadow and Green Hills clubs near San Francisco and the Valley Club at Santa Barbara.

They formed an association, named it the MacKenzie Society, and held their inaugural annual club competition in 1987 at the Valley Club at Montecito on the Pacific coast north west of Los Angeles.

Little did they know it at the time, but those pioneers had set in train an organisation and an annual gathering that would girdle the globe with 15 member clubs in Great Britain, Ireland, Australia, New Zealand, Canada and even South America.

In the early days the competition rotated annually between the four founding clubs. But in 1992, Crystal Downs from Michigan and California's Cypress Point were admitted to the society. The following year Lahinch in Ireland's County Clare became the first overseas member.

In the next five years, expansion continued briskly with the inclusion of Australia's Royal Melbourne and Eire's Cork (1995), The St. Charles Country Club in Winnipeg (1997) and, in 1998, Moortown, Alwoodley and New Zealand's Titirangi. Claremont, from Oakland in California, came on board in 2002 and, intriguingly, the Jockey Club of Buenos Aires, Argentina, in 2007.

The form of the competition is that of an 8-man team made up of the club professional, the club champion, the MacKenzie Director, the club historian and four handicap golfers playing in flights of handicaps from scratch to 18.

The trophy for which they compete is known as the MacKenzie Cup and, fittingly, it recalls the doctor's Scottish ancestry: a set of bagpipes mounted on a plinth with the names of the winning teams engraved on a silver plaque.

The bagpipes, however, have been enthusiastically handled down the years. So much so that when the competition came to Moortown in 2005, the pipes were judged to be too delicate to cross the Atlantic and were represented instead by a life-size colour photograph.

Some of the teams that have represented Moortown over the years, from Left to Right

1998 Pasatiempo – Len Fawke, Roger Eames, Keith Wheelhouse, Jack Cooke, Jeff Smith, Vince Green, Chris Lord, Peter Rogerson

2000 Royal Melbourne – Geoff Mortimer, Guy Bradley, Jack Cooke, Peter Hart, Richard Hurst, Bryon Hutchinson, Len Fawke and Colin Gaines

2001 Crystal Down Team – Chris Lord, Robert Westmoreland, Richard Brown, Ian Watts, Jack Cooke, Ken Spencer, Geoff Mortimer, and Richard Hurst

2002 Meadow Club – Bryon Hutchinson, Richard Brown, Chris Craven, Peter Rogerson, Roger Eames, Colin Gaines, Jack Cooke, Ken Spencer.

2003 GreenHills – Malcolm Slinger, Peter Rogerson, Don McClennan, Geoff Mortimer, Ken Spencer, Roger Eames, Ian Watts and Martin Heggie

2004 St Charles – Len Fawke, Martin Heggie, Peter Rogerson, Don McClennan, Richard Brown, Ian Hartley, Jack Cooke and Geoff Flint.

2005 Moortown and Alwoodley – Martin Heggie, Stephen East, Richard Brown, Colin Gaines, Fred Davies, Tim Russell, Peter Rogerson and Tom Hurley.

2006 Valley Club – Tim Russell, Clive Bowyer, Peter Rogerson, Martin Heggie, Bill Holmes, Malcolm Slinger, Fred Davies and Geoff Mortimer.

2007 Cypress Point – Martin Heggie, Peter Rogerson, Captain David Sheret, Ian Chippendale, Back Tim Russell, Richard Mapplebeck, David Powers, John Bruce

The MacKenzie Cup Bagpipe Trophy

Moortown's involvement in the MacKenzie Society started ten years earlier when the then Captain, Vince Green, received a letter from the Society asking if he would like to attend their next gathering in Lahinch as an observer. At the time, Moortown's knowledge of the MacKenzie Society was scant but Vince instinctively sensed that this might be an opportunity too good to miss. He speedily accepted their invitation. What he saw at Lahinch made him more and more enthusiastic about the format of the event, the opportunities for Moortown and the spirit of international camaraderie which hallmarked the annual gathering. A few months later a letter bearing the now familiar MacKenzie Society logo arrived, inviting Vince Green to become the MacKenzie Director for Moortown and to confirm Moortown's membership of the Society. Subsequently the Club received an official invitation to play in the 1998 event at Pasatiempo.

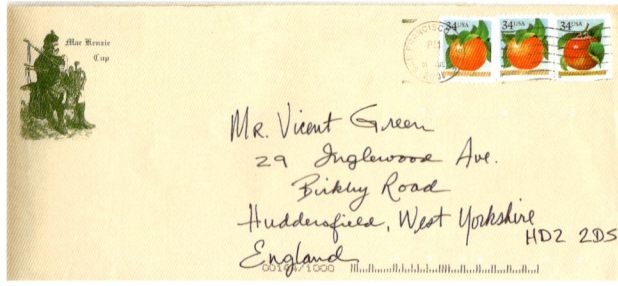

Vince Green's invitation letter

1998 - 2004

It would be difficult to think of a more appropriate setting than Santa Cruz in California for Moortown to make its MacKenzie Cup debut. Not only was Pasatiempo one of the founders of the Society, it was also where Alister MacKenzie made his final home, overlooking the 6th fairway, a location that was to provide a particular treat for the Moortown team a few days after they arrived.

Pasatiempo 1998
Moortown members in front of the Bagpipes Trophy

Though the house had been sold after his death in 1934, the current owners maintained the MacKenzie connection by inviting all the competitors to a cocktail party. It was held on the lawn overlooking the course and, poignantly, not far from where the doctor's open-air funeral had been held near the 6th fairway and where his ashes had been scattered on the course.

But first, and prior to the official event, the Moortown players were to enjoy one of golf's most exclusive privileges - a round at the MacKenzie-designed Cypress Point. Moortown was one of several overseas teams invited to Cypress which itself was competing in the annual MacKenzie Trophy.

On the last day of the MacKenzie competition proper, an elaborately choreographed prize-giving was conducted on the terrace of the clubhouse where most of the US teams were smartly attired in team strips. The Moortown new boys, however, were sporting the widest variety of golf shirts imaginable. Needless to say, since that day forth, Moortown has always travelled with sufficient kit to ensure that co-ordinated Moortown team shirts would be worn on the final day. As for the competition, the winning team was the home club, Pasatiempo.

Pasatiempo 1998
The Moortown Team at the prize giving

Cypress Point, were second and, in line with another MacKenzie Cup tradition, all the other teams were equal third.

Twelve months later a Moortown team returned to California to The Valley Club at Santa Barbara. As an appetiser, they played first at Spyglass Hill in Monterey. Named after "Treasure Island" whose author Robert Louis Stevenson knew the area well, Spyglass was to create the first of two memorable Moortown moments that year. Vince Green

Cec Bloice, Vince Green, Chris Lord and Len Fawke at the
15th hole at Cypress Point on the 1999 Valley Club trip

managed to par a hole with the forbidding title of Black Dog, one of the most difficult holes in California, let alone at Spyglass. Flushed with success, Vince acquired a golf cap emblazoned with the words "Black Dog" - a nickname by which he's been known by ever since.

The final day at Valley was enlivened when one Moortown member, Peter Rogerson, holed in one; the first to have been recorded in the history of the competition. Learning of his feat, the Australians from Royal Melbourne were quick (and loud) to make much mileage out of the tradition of drinks all round at the expense of the scorer. But tradition clashed with reality because at the time a free bar was in full swing and, in any event, Valley was a cashless club in which only members could sign for drinks. A diplomatic incident with Australia was narrowly averted when, exceptionally, it was agreed that a tab could be created and the bill posted to Peter at Moortown. The old country's face had thus been saved while the Australians were much mollified at the sight of a team of waiters passing out glasses of champagne as quickly as they could be poured. Honour had been satisfied all round.

There were no such feats a year later when Royal Melbourne hosted the event, though Moortown, doubtless assisted by the inaugural presence on the team of the club pro, Bryon Hutchinson, did record their best-ever competition performance: a genuine third place.

The 2001 event was staged in Michigan, USA. The most northerly of the US MacKenzie clubs, Crystal Downs is snowbound for five months or so each year and the course was due to close for the winter not along after the competition. But the occasion was heavily overshadowed by 9/11 which took place the day before the event. With the grounding of commercial flights throughout the United States, some teams were unable to get there. And, for the same reason, many of those who did manage to arrive, were unable to return home. Crystal Down's pro, Fred Muller, arranged open-ended motel accommodation for the Moortown team as well as unlimited, gratis use of the course. But, as it turned out, the team's flight was one of a handful not to be cancelled that weekend. After two rigorous searches of themselves and their baggage by armed troops from the US National Guard, the team left Chicago's O'Hare Airport for Manchester - one of only three commercial flights in US airspace that day.

The competition in 2002, held at The Meadow Club in the hills north of San Francisco, marked the debut of Peter Rogerson as Moortown's new MacKenzie Director following Vince Green's retirement. 2002 also marked the final appearance in the competition of Moortown's longstanding pro, Bryon Hutchinson, who retired before the next event. His successor, Martin Heggie, duly made his MacKenzie debut a year later in 2003 at the Green Hills Club which is just 20 minutes from San Francisco's bustling financial centre and Silicon Valley.

Nowhere was the global reach of Moortown members more in evidence than in Canada in 2004 when the host was the St. Charles Country Club in Winnipeg. Stopping off first in

The Moortown team in front of their stretch limo at Toronto

Toronto, the team was met by the former Moortown member, Sean O'Hara, son of the late Terry O'Hara, past president, past chairman and past captain of Moortown. As a Toronto resident, Sean organised golf, restaurants and transport in some style, even down to providing Moortown with their own stretch limo for their entire stay as well as golf at two wonderful courses nearby, Devil's Pulpit and the National. St Charles put

Valley Club 1999 - Vince Green MacKenzie Director highlighting Peter Rogerson's hole in one

The Moortown team relaxing after their round at St Charles in 2004

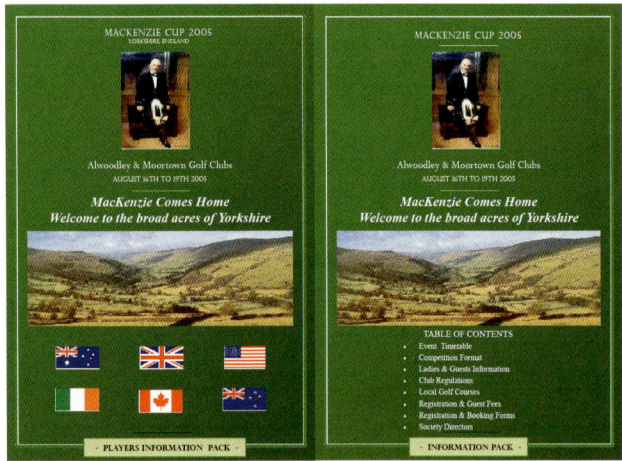

Moortown 2005 - The Registration and Information pack

Moortown 2005 - The traditional Scottish Pipers performing before the Men's Dinner

on a great event with their clubhouse capable of dining 300 guests with a team of chefs headed by Takashi Murakami one of the top chefs in Canada. Fittingly St Charles were the tournament winners with Moortown the runners up.

2005 MOORTOWN AND ALWOODLEY GOLF CLUBS, LEEDS

This was a vintage year for Moortown and its near neighbour, Alwoodley – the sole British member clubs of the MacKenzie Society whose Board decided that the 2005 competition should be held in the UK for the first time in its history. As the two clubs were so close to each other, it was further decided that the event should be co-hosted by them – another first in the life of the MacKenzie Society.

The joint organising committee quickly decided that because of co-hosting, the competition should be extended to a 4-day event with a practice round and a competition round at both clubs to be held between August 16th and 19th. It was also decided that the profile and presentation of the event should be accorded a high priority both before and during the event. In this respect, the bar had been raised by the 2004 hosts, St Charles Country Club of Winnipeg. Accordingly the two Leeds clubs produced a glossy, picture-rich publication entitled "MacKenzie Comes Home" as a comprehensive guide for their guests.

In the year of the competition itself, there was a special televised curtain raiser a few days before the event began: Harry Gration, the popular local television presenter of BBC Look North (and a keen golfer in his own right) was invited play Moortown's most famous hole, Gibraltar, in the company of Peter Rogerson, Martin Heggie and Nick Leefe, Peter's opposite number at Alwoodley. In addition, Yorkshire Television's evening news magazine, Calendar, was at Alwoodley to broadcast coverage of the final day's play.

A related event generated considerable publicity in the regional morning newspaper, The Yorkshire Post, and its evening stablemate, The Yorkshire Evening Post. This arose from an innovative initiative from Ian Watts, a past captain and current committee man at Moortown. He wondered if MacKenzie's house - less than a mile or so from the two clubs - could win recognition with the award of the coveted blue plaque indicating a building of historic interest.

An approach was made to the Leeds Civic Trust, the awarding body, which, after proper consideration, agreed that the golfing doctor's house on the corner of Lidgett Lane and Harrogate Road met the necessary criteria. The present owners of the house, now a local residents' club, had earlier been canvassed and were happy for a plaque to be installed on the wall of their property. Additionally, the owners entered fully into the spirit of the event with their willingness to receive any American visitors who wished to see a piece of MacKenzie memorabilia for themselves.

Moortown 2005 - International flags flying over the starters hut

Moortown 2005 - MacKenzie Cup scorecard

In keeping with the tradition of MacKenzie Cups, two Scottish pipers were engaged to appear in full regalia at the week's social events. Their first engagement was to greet players, wives, partners and guests as they arrived in the glow of a warm sunlit evening for Wednesday's formal welcoming cocktail party at Harewood House. The presence at the party of Lord Harewood himself and the historic setting of the formal gardens and terraces added greatly to the ambience of what was a uniquely English occasion.

Nor were the needs of players' partners and guests overlooked. The lady members of the organising committee arranged a Ladies' Dinner at the Sun Pavilion at Valley Gardens in Harrogate, a visit to Castle Howard, a coach trip to the Bronte Country and daily visits hosted by the ladies of Moortown and Alwoodley.

The event proper started on the morning of the 17th with the first practice round at Alwoodley, starting at the 1st tee, playing in 4-ball groups, made up of two players from two clubs in their appropriate flights. At 9am the following morning, after all the teams' equipment and the golf buggies had been transferred overnight from Alwoodley, a further practice round, similar to the previous day's at Alwoodley, followed.

Drinks before the Men's Dinner

Moortown provided 20 dedicated team hosts, drawn from the ranks of members who had played previously in the competition. The hosts were assigned to the teams throughout their time at Moortown and proved to be great ambassadors for the club.

The competition began in earnest the following day, Thursday the 18th. After the annual ritual of team photographs, the first

Hosts assembled to await the competitors

Geoff Mortimer and Len Fawke at the Half Way House

Dining Room before the Men's Dinner

round began with a shotgun start at Moortown. The format was modified greensome (Pinehurst); teams in flights as normal; Stableford full handicap allowance; professionals and champions playing off white tees; the remainder off yellow tees.

That evening a further cocktail party for the players plus a sprinkling of honoured guests was held in the Club Marquee at Moortown followed by the Men's Dinner in the clubhouse. The guest speaker was the lawyer and golfer, Ian Shuttleworth, with a bravura performance of Yorkshire humour.

The final day's competition was at Alwoodley on Friday the 16th. The format was as at Moortown but a betterball 4-ball Stableford. The day - and the event - then concluded with a finger buffet and prize presentation ceremony. The winners, Crystal Downs were formally handed a giant photograph of the trophy, as the original was deemed too frail to travel. Moortown finished a creditable second.

Not to be forgotten that evening was an impromptu performance of the traditional Maori haka by members of New Zealand's Titirangi Club. Though short on Maori performers, the team was long on fierce faces, wild gesticulations and a turn of showmanship which did their country proud.

2006 - 2008

2006's competition at The Valley Club in Santa Barbara was the first time that Moortown had revisited a MacKenzie venue and, again, the team and partners arrived in San Francisco, drove down the Pacific coastline to Carmel and started the weekend by playing Cypress Point on the Saturday and Spy Glass on the Sunday. The organisers had decided to change the normal format by having three days of competition rather than a practice day and two days of competition. But once again the Americans in their own back yard were just too powerful and were more than capable of contending with the fast US greens. Moortown came away with only the satisfaction of having defeated their old rivals, Alwoodley.

In 2007 the jewel in the MacKenzie Society's crown, Cypress Point, played host for the first time at their legendary course. Cypress must surely be the only venue that can insist on caddies for all players. Even though they double bagged, 60 experienced caddies were provided for all the teams.

Valley Club 2006, team and partners at the prizegiving

The Moortown team and the famous trophy

Moortown's first meeting with the obligatory caddies was at the practice round where the benefits of their services soon became apparent. Mostly single figure golfers themselves, the caddies had an intimate knowledge of the entire course. Although some teams had differing caddies for the main event, Moortown deftly arranged to retain the same caddies for the three days, thus building up friendship and confidence in their selection of clubs and the best lines on the greens. After the first round, Moortown lay promisingly in sixth place, but slipped back in the final round. The local team triumphed convincingly with Meadow Club in second place.

2008 AUSTRALIA AND NEW ZEALAND

In 2008 Moortown went down under with their largest-ever MacKenzie party to contest the competition in Titirangi, New Zealand. The 22 members and partners were hosted en route by Royal Melbourne Golf Club. Their hospitality arrangements included two days of golf at their famous club, a day at the races to see the Melbourne Cup, plus seats at the Rugby League World Cup match between England and Australia, and a further round of golf at Kingston Heath, Australia's second most famous golf course.

From there the party moved on to New Zealand's South Island playing golf at the Clearwater Resort at Christchurch and at the magnificent Arrowtown course, set in the snowcapped mountains near Queenstown. The party then flew to the North Island playing at Cape Kidnappers - rated as the best course in New Zealand - before arriving at Auckland for the main event at Titirangi. The club had recently spent NZ$5 million on the course and it was a superb test of golf. Unfortunately it proved too big a test for Moortown who lost their usual wager to their old rivals Alwoodley.

Over the years, 40 Moortown members have represented their club in the competition whose roll of honour includes 11 captains, 2 professionals and 2 directors. Places on the team are hotly contested, but those who win through are rewarded with the special camaraderie that goes with the contest as well as the opportunity to play some memorable courses and the chance to form some great golfing friendships around the world.

2008 Moortown team wives on their way to the Melbourne Cup, Susan Russell, Rosemary Mortimer, Jane Slinger, Lindsay Rogerson and Yvonne Brown.

2008 Titirangi GC - MacKenzie team - Back Row: David Marriott, Martin Heggie, Malcolm Slinger, David Earnshaw, Front Row Bob Seaton, Geoff Mortimer, Graham Etherington and Peter Rogerson

2008 MacKenzie Cup the Titirangi Registration Desk

2008 Titirangi, Maori dance before tee off

Christie O'Connor 'Himself' Driving off the 1st at the Ryder Cup Memories Day

XII MILLENNIUM FESTIVAL WEEK

When the golf historians of the future look back on the life and times of Moortown, it's likely that the club's celebration of the millennium will stand out as one of its landmarks. A variety of schemes to herald 'Moortown's Millennium' were proposed, sifted, and assessed. But the club finally chose to mark the new century by celebrating and updating what was arguably Moortown's finest moment from the old century - the staging of the Ryder Cup in 1929.

But speed was of the essence. By late 1999 when the idea took root, there was little lead time left to get an ambitious scheme off the ground. And schemes don't come much more ambitious than the prospect of a first-ever royal visit to Moortown.

This arose from an approach to HRH The Duke of York by Roger Eames, the Club's then Vice Captain who worked for The Outward Bound Trust whose Management Committee was chaired by HRH.

Prince Andrew was delighted to agree in principle to attend, but the not inconsiderable hurdle of securing a mutually convenient date needed to be overcome. By now planning was well under way for a 7-day festival of golf under the banner of Ryder Cup Memories Week. The date pencilled in was the period in June in which Captain's Day was traditionally held. The club's strong preference therefore was that the Royal visit should take place during that week.

Unfortunately, however, Prince Andrew was placed on standby for a military visit at that time and, as events turned out, he ended up meeting troops in Bosnia rather than Ryder Cup golfers at Moortown! Though the prospect of a Royal visit had been an attractive one, the Club regrettably had to abandon the idea. Disappointing though this was, the club's outgoing President, Victor Watson, suggested that the Duke's absence did not mean that the club also had to abandon the notion of a celebratory week.

THE PLANNING

It was immediately apparent that a successful corporate golf day would be key to the week's success. It was equally clear that it would have to be a top quality event if financial commitments were to be won from those in the corporate sector. That, in turn, would go a long way towards meeting the substantial costs of staging the festival – notably the hire of two vast marquees.

Frank Prust, Club Captain Roger Eames, Christie O'Connor & Victor Watson

The framework of the festival having been agreed and the dates having been confirmed as June 11th to June 17th, detailed planning began in earnest. One of the early decisions was to increase the profile of the event by commissioning a special Ryder Cup Memories logo for use on merchandise and publicity material. Another was to strengthen the organising committee by bringing on board the "in-club" expertise of one of its members, Gerry Connolly, who had unrivalled expertise in the staging of corporate golf and PGA events.

Moortown's Ryder Cup Memories Day Logo

The priority, however, was selecting and perfecting the theme for the corporate day. The winning idea was to mark the club's heritage as a Ryder Cup venue with a Ryder Cup Memories Day. Invitations were extended to all European Ryder Cup players past and present to reunite at Moortown and participate in the corporate golf day.

The first to be invited was the legendary Christie O'Connor, "Himself". His rapid acceptance prompted many more Ryder Cup players to follow suit. There was no appearance money on offer, or 'pro prizes'. But the attractiveness of the idea, the chance to rekindle their Ryder Cup experiences, the opportunity to meet up with old friends (plus the payment of accommodation and travelling expenses) was sufficient to draw some distinguished players to Moortown, none more so than Mark James, the reigning European Ryder Cup captain.

The legendary Christie O'Connor 'Himself' on the Moortown putting green

Meanwhile the timetable for the week was firmly taking shape: a major event was pencilled in for each of the seven days, beginning with a Moortown Men's Members' Day and a Moortown Ladies' Invitation Day on Monday and Tuesday respectively. The week's signature event, the Corporate Day, would follow on the Wednesday with another major competition, an International Club Team Competition, on Thursday the 15th.

The course would be given a rest on the Friday, but not the marquee. It would be the setting for a Sportsman's Lunch and an afternoon of entertainment on the lighter side of sporting life. The curtain would finally be brought down on Saturday the 17th with two traditional events: Captain's Day golf followed by a black-tie ball.

SPONSORS' NIGHT

Invitations were sent to a number of companies (many of whose executives were Moortown members) to attend a sponsor's night presentation in February 2000 when the plans for the day would be unveiled. By the end of

Members relaxing in the sunshine after their round prior to the presentation dinner

the evening, the corporate golf day had been fully sold out – due in no small measure to Gerry Connolly's vivid big screen presentation. The many doubters among the club membership, who thought the costs of entering a team were unrealistically high, stood corrected. In addition to selling out all the corporate spots, a main sponsor, Standard Fireworks, was also secured that evening and, it's worth noting, all this was achieved even in advance of signing up a full roster of Ryder cup players.

THE MARQUEE

Given that the organisers were planning a series of black-tie and luncheon events with 300 to 400 guests, it was clear that the clubhouse facilities alone would be inadequate to cope with such large numbers. Accordingly, two huge linked marquees were hired to be erected at the side of the 18th fairway.

But then a complication arose with the need to accommodate a large gorse bush at the edge of the fairway. Though not particularly attractive, the bush was an integral feature of the course and could be seen on old photographs. As the organisers had no wish to contend with the ire of the head greenkeeper, Bill Fox, the contractor was required to offset the two marquees in order to fit the gorse bush in between them – of course, at additional cost and inconvenience.

Ironically, it only emerged later that Bill Fox was no lover of the bush either and would have been quite happy had it been removed. Needless to say, the offending gorse is no longer there.

MEN'S AND LADY MEMBERS' DAY

The marquee was duly erected, and the first event hosted was the Men's Members' Day on Monday, June 12th. But it was a close run thing. While the players were out on the course, hectic last minute work was still under way in the marquee to erect the bar and set up the optics and beer pumps. At the same time there was a staffing hiccough which threatened the orderly proceedings still further. The bar steward, Len, had reported sick the previous day and was unavailable for the rest of the week. A bevy of young ladies were drafted in, including the chairman's daughter, and they coped like professionals throughout the week. The day's golf, a Men's Members' 4 ball Am-Am with a shotgun start, was followed by a Presentation Dinner in the marquee. The Ryder Cup Memories Week had successfully begun and on the following day, Tuesday 13th, it was the ladies' turn and they held an Invitation Greensomes Stableford Competition.

RYDER CUP MEMORIES CORPORATE DAY

Altogether 15 former Ryder Cup players accepted their invitations which delighted the committee, particularly as the Moortown event clashed with the US Open. As a result, some Ryder Cup players had regretfully declined because they had already accepted television commitments in the United States. Tour players and some local pros were invited to take their places.

The Ryder Cup players headed by Christie O'Connor Senior (10 Ryder Cup appearances) were Mark James, who had captained the European Ryder Cup Team at Brookline the previous September and who had 7 appearances; Maurice Bembridge (1969,71,73,75); John Garner (1971,73); Gordon J Brand (1983); Norman Drew (1959); Lionel Platts (1965); Peter Townsend (1969,71); Harry Bannerman (1971); Norman Wood (1975); Des Smyth (1979,81); Antonio Garrido (1979): Michael King (1979), Brian Waites (1983) and John O'Leary (1975).

The Marquee split in two to accommodate the gorse bush

For the organisers, one of the day's earliest requirements had an unexpected outcome. It arose from the filling of a convoy of 70 golf buggies at the nearby petrol station on Harrogate Road. But, because each buggy's tankfull had to be paid for separately, the multiple swipes of the credit card eventually caused it to be refused. Thus the morning rush hour on Harrogate Road was brought to a standstill.

A couple of hours later, light drizzle greeted the players as they began to arrive at the club. Spirits, however, were high, not least because of the popular champagne breakfast held in the marquee for the 35 competing teams. The list of sponsors read like a roll call of Yorkshire's industrial, commercial and business leaders and included BT, Cisco, Unisys, Aon, PriceWaterhouseCoopers, and, of course, the week's sponsor, Standard Fireworks.

The competition began with starts at the 1st and 9th. The first game off the first tee was Moortown's professional, Bryon Hutchinson, who was under strict instructions to pace himself and not to arrive at the ninth until the teams starting there had teed off. Meanwhile the first game off the 9th tee was led by Jack Cooke, Moortown's MacKenzie historian and Chairman of its House Committee.

Also at the 9th was a luxury motor home dispensing refreshments and pastries provided by one of the club's members, Martyn Ainsley, in what proved to be a convivial meeting place for players and followers alike. However, relaxing as this was, it was vital that teams adhered to the timetable if all 35 were to complete their rounds, have a drink or two, shower and change in time for a 7.00pm Champagne Reception in the Memories Garden Bar followed by the Gala Dinner and prize presentation in the marquee.

There was a very full agenda that night which was attended by over 350 players, wives and VIP guests. After the dinner

Martyn Ainsley with Christie O'Connor

The scoreboard welcoming the teams before play

Refreshments at the Motorhome at the 9th Tee

Ian Chippindale sharing a pastry with John Garner

Christie with Club Chairman Peter Rogerson and Don Hanley

Club Members Simon Stephens and John Anderson relaxing with Mark James before their round

Maurice Bembridge getting ready to tee off the 1st with Peter Holmes

Mark James driving off the 1st in the 2000 Ryder Cup Memories Day

Christie O'Connor driving off watched by Victor Watson and Roger Eames

The Ryder Cup players assembled after the dinner

The Winning Pro-am Team of Stephenson Group's Richard Bentley and Club Pro John Hammond

and prize presentation, the Ryder Cup players were called on to the stage where a memento presentation was made to them by the club captain together with a vote of thanks for their attendance. Peter Townsend responded with well chosen anecdotes from his Ryder cup matches with Harry Bannerman. This was followed by a screening of a televised Ryder Cup history (including shots of some of those present). There was then a memorabilia auction for Martin House Hospice.

Another of the evening's highlights was the award of Honorary Club membership to Mark James, the first non-member to receive this award since Walter Hagen after the 1929 Ryder Cup.

However, the full programme had taken its toll and by late evening the schedule could be kept up no longer. As a result the huge, lengthy and outstanding firework display (courtesy of the event sponsor, Standard Fireworks) began very late that night which, in turn, was followed by a cabaret singer, dancers and a band playing into the early hours.

All this was not altogether to the liking of several - indeed, many - of the club's neighbouring residents. This was underlined by the arrival at 3.00am of a police sergeant inquiring when the party might end and if that might be any time soon. Knowing troubled waters when he saw them, the habitually emollient chairman, Peter Rogerson, decided to withdraw himself from the following day's International Club Team competition. The club's best interests, he surmised, could best be served by leaving his clubs in the locker room to spend an hour or two in the secretary's office applying soothing oil to those residents who had rung, in various degrees of irritation, to register their discontent.

INTERNATIONAL TEAM CLUB COMPETTIION

The 24 clubs invited to this popular event were either Ryder Cup venues, or MacKenzie courses in the UK and Ireland, or local clubs which competed with Moortown for club team trophies. There was a particularly warm welcome for the Worcester Country Club team who made the trip from New England in the United States, the first Ryder Cup venue in the

The Fulford team playing in the International Club Competition

US. Other Ryder Cup host clubs represented at Moortown were Ganton, Lindrick, and Royal Birkdale. MacKenzie course clubs included Alwoodley, Bingley (St Ives), Cork, Lahinch, Sand Moor, Ilkley and Oakdale. One club, the Menwith Hill Golf Society, had the unique distinction of being a US club based in the UK.

The day's play, a 4-ball am-am team championship, was followed by a cocktail party in the Ryder Cup Memories Garden Bar. The presentation dinner was held in the Marquee where once again Victor Watson, Moortown's immediate Past President, demonstrated just why he is such a sought-after dinner speaker throughout the North of England.

SPORTSMANS LUNCH & TRICK SHOT GOLF

Friday was a day of rest and recreation; rest for the course from competitive play and recreation for members and their guests. Organised by the club's vice-captain, Geoff Mortimer, the Sportsman's Lunch in the Marquee featured a dry, witty and knowledgeable speech from one of the game's elder statesman, John Sterling, a former captain of the PGA and ex head coach at the English Golf Union. The afternoon was warm, still and sunny - perfect conditions for an hilarious demonstration of trick shot golf by David Edwards from Lincolnshire's Forest Pines Golf Club, though, halfway through his performance, even he might have been startled to witness Bert Budin's approach to the 18th when the course was not exactly closed, but its use was being strongly discouraged.

The final element of the afternoon's entertainment brought an unusual sight to the 18th fairway: a well-upholstered all-girl trio who sang and danced for the edification of those who had repaired to the garden bar as the day's proceedings drew to a close.

MOORTOWN CAPTAIN'S DAY & MILLENNIUM BALL

The final day of Moortown's festival of golf, dawned with more fine and sunny weather for the traditional Captain's Day Members Men's Competition. Members teed off from 7.30 a.m, stopping at the Halfway House for traditional drinks and snacks with the Captain, Roger Eames, while a scoreboard at the 18th green recorded the fortunes of every player. After the golf, 435 members, wives and guests assembled for a cocktail party prior to the black-tie Millennium Ball which rounded off both the day and the week. Also included were the traditional formal club photographs of men and lady members gathered in front of the clubhouse in the evening sunshine.

After the dinner, a unique cabaret devised by Victor Watson acted out a pageant of the history of Moortown from MacKenzie's days to the present and featured several be-costumed members – much to the amusement of the assembled company.

A scheduled firework display by the sponsor, Standard Fireworks, was judiciously sidelined lest the display rekindled the ire of Wednesday's complainants who had been so effectively mollified by the Chairman.

Guests arrive at the Cocktail Party before the Ball

The Marquee in readiness for the Ball

Shelagh Day. Didi Powers with Past Lady Captains Ailsa Jarvis and Linda Hudson at the Millennium Ball

Paul & Ann Sellars, Dave & Kay Sayers, Gerry Connolly, Caroline Learoyd, Chris & Jo Lord at the ball.

A section of the Members lining up for the Millennium Club Photograph

Moortown's Ladies in Centenary Edwardian Dress

XIII THE LADIES

There can be few, if any, clubs whose most famous – and valuable - trophy is firmly in the ownership of the ladies section. Moortown's ladies, however, have that unique distinction and have held it since 1929.

After the 1929 Ryder Cup, Sam Ryder presented the ladies with a "Ryder Commemoration Trophy" in appreciation of the help given by the ladies during the competition. According to a letter from Miss Ryder in 1960, who was present with her father in 1929, no other Club has such a trophy. The ladies must indeed have excelled themselves in their assistance to those involved in the matches. A fulsome letter of appreciation to Mrs Butler was received from the Hon. Secretary of the Professional Golfers' Association, Mr Percy Perrins, thanking the ladies for their "organisation in the Committee Room and all they did for the comfort and convenience of Committee Members and the British Team".

Their efforts at the Ryder Cup seem typical of the active part played by women in the club's history. But formal written records of their achievements in the very early years are scant. It is a matter of record that there have been lady captains from 1910 and that inter-club matches were held as early as 1911. But, apart from the odd reference in the General Committee minutes, little else is known of the early female pioneers.

However, from 1921 onwards, proper minutes were maintained of the ladies' proceedings. Right from the start they demonstrate the enduring qualities of Moortown's decision-making: the very first reference in the new minutes was to arrange a date for the annual Captain v. Secretary's match - a fixture still contested today. The officials at that time were the Lady Captain who, as now, acted as Chairman of the ladies' committee, the Ex-Captain, who remained on the committee for one year after captaincy, Treasurer, Secretary and six committee members. Members of committee were elected for three years and were not eligible for re-election for one year afterwards. The Lady Captain was nominated by the committee and voted on at the A.G.M. to act as Vice for one year. For some reason there was no Vice-Captain's role after 1933 until it was reinstated in 1951. This must have made it difficult for a newly elected member to take office with no prior training or experience. However, from 1952 onwards a Vice-Captain was appointed and was involved in committee matters, and in later years acted as captain of the 'B' team.

During the war years there was an arrangement that in the event of severe air raids 50–100 homeless would be housed temporarily in the clubhouse until billets were provided. Equipment and rations would be stored in the small card room. Volunteers were requested to help and Miss Pollard would lead the team. Thankfully, there was only one occasion overnight when the facilities were needed for mothers and babies, which was during the flying bomb attacks in 1944. A Yorkshire Post group photograph shows these evacuees and Moortown ladies who were acting as volunteer helpers.

The W.V.S. asked if the ladies would work on camouflage netting to assist the war effort, and large frames were set up in the main lounge and present T.V. room. The ladies had to weave strips of different shades of material through the netting, and many hours were spent on this work. At the end of the war 2,000 large nets had been completed and sent away for use by the military. There was also a knitting circle

Moortown Members
Miss Greenwood, 2. Mrs Smithson, 3. Mrs Walkland,
4. Miss Pollard, 5. Mrs Sley, 6. Mrs Foreman,
7. Mrs Butler, 8. Mrs Jeken

and wool fund to provide gloves, scarves and balaclavas, but this had to be abandoned due to wool rationing in 1941. Money was sent to club employees in the Forces instead. By October 1945 all the wartime equipment from the small card room had been cleared and the room could be used for bridge again.

In 1948, rather than the committee putting forward a nominee for Captain to be voted on at the A.G.M., it was agreed that a sub-committee comprising the Captain and a number of ex-captains should meet to make the choice.

In 1953 it was decided to present the Captain with a silver ash tray as a memento of her year in office. This custom continued until 1990, when it was considered that a small silver Armada dish would be more suitable for the future. In 1980 the Club committee granted Lady Captains honorary membership during their year of office. Currently the Lady Captain is also the custodian of an attractive gold captain's brooch.

Up to the end of World War II competitions were played during the day, and prizes presented the same afternoon. However, the committee were anxious not to exclude the increasing number of those who worked during the week from participating in competitions, and from 1946, in a decision which was well in advance of many other clubs, they decided that those members should be allowed to play on the evening of the competition day during the summer, with prizes presented at the end of the year. In 1957 the committee made the final decision that Medals and Bogeys could be played on Sundays, thus allowing all working ladies to play in all competitions.

In 1987 it was decided that, rather than the Captain, Secretary and occasionally Vice-Captain, considering applications for membership, this could be devolved on to a small membership sub-committee consisting of experienced and long-standing members who would interview prospective members and make recommendations to the general committee. This proved satisfactory and has continued ever since.

Lady Captain's Brooch

The system for electing all members at Moortown included recommendations from two sponsors from the men's section. This made it difficult for ladies who knew no male members to be accepted. The ladies' committee had requested several times over the years the right to propose and second lady applicants, and in 2003 this was finally agreed, with the ladies' committee taking responsibility for the suitability of the member.

The A.G.M. is the most important business meeting of the year and has always been held on the last Saturday in November. It was a very full day as after the business meeting held in the afternoon, when the major trophies were also presented, there was a hot supper or dinner, followed by an evening Bridge Drive. From 1957, however, it was decided to hold a separate A.G.M. at the end of November, preceded by an annual dinner and trophy and prize presentation earlier in the month as the last social function of the golf year. This proved most successful and has continued ever since.

The 2008 AGM Meeting when Caroline Learoyd handed over the captaincy to Centenary Captain Adele Allan

Afternoon tea in the ladies lounge

In 1954 it was decided that any matters members wished to raise at the A.G.M. should be notified in writing at least ten days prior to the meeting. Before this, members were inclined to raise contentious issues under 'Any Other Business', which caused arguments and long discussions at the meeting.

Early in 2004 there was a suggestion that the ladies' year end be changed from the traditional November, which coincided with the Y.L.C.G.A. year, to the end of February when the men's year ended. An Extraordinary General Meeting was called and there was a vote in favour of change. During the summer, however, there was much discussion among members over the wisdom of having passed this resolution, and for several reasons many considered that the traditional year end should have been retained. Eventually it was decided to call a second E.G.M. and after further discussion, the original resolution was rescinded and the November year end retained.

The question of dress in the clubhouse had never been an issue amongst the ladies. The practice was for competitors to change after playing and suitability was not in question. However, in 1964 ladies occasionally wore trousers in the lounge and this caused some comment so the committee decided that "ladies are requested to refrain from wearing trousers in the sun lounge". Time and fashion moved on and by 1969 it was agreed that "trouser suits can be worn in the sun lounge". In about 2000 there was a radical relaxation of the dress code for both men and ladies and "smart casual" was allowed in the clubhouse until 7pm.

On the course in times past ladies wore skirts for golf and there was no interest in anything fashionable. In fact skirts were even rolled up or hung on hooks in lockers with golf clubs. Gradually clothing firms began to take an interest in the golfing scene and today most attractive wear is available in all colours and styles. It would be interesting to know how the men members view this transformation. Perhaps they do not approve if this complaint in 1991 is anything to go by. The ladies' committee were officially informed that the men "are concerned at the wearing of tight trousers with ties under the feet". Our committee did not quite understand this, but promised to keep a watchful eye on tight trousers.

Competitions

Competitive golf has always played the major part of life at Moortown. Membership was greater in the early days as records show 100–130, but although it has varied since it now seems established at about 90–100. Numbers entering competitions have not, however, changed much, but Medals and Stablefords are not as popular today, perhaps partly due to other commitments. The rules for entering competitions were very strict in the 1920s, and the ladies had to work hard at their golf. At least one card per month had to be returned to make a player eligible for a competition. In match play, until 1954, if there was a tie after 18 holes a further 18 had to be played, and in 1947 one knockout match was even played four times before there was a result! No sheltering was allowed in any competition. The knock-out finals were over 36 holes. Draws were made for all competitions except Medals and Bogeys "to mix members". It was decreed in 1935 that if there was a tie in a 36-hole competition a further 36 had to be played. These rules were naturally somewhat relaxed as the years went by.

The par of the course was originally 79, reduced to 77 in 1921 and further reduced to 76 in 1931. In 1947 the L.G.U. made a reduction to 74 which caused the committee to protest strongly at such a drastic step. The L.G.U. relented and there was a concession to 75 for "course difficulties". This S.S.S. remains today.

In 1998, however, Handicaps were calculated by a new computer system which was more complicated and initially caused much discussion. It has taken several years for some members to accustom themselves to this new system, which does, nevertheless, provide a more accurate picture of a player's current form.

The fixture list for the following year is prepared with the new captain after the November A.G.M., and it can be said that there are competitions to include all standards of golf. Trophies and cups have been presented to the section over the years, either donated or purchased to commemorate a member or mark a special event. The format of the competitions has in some instances never changed since inception, but others have been modified over time for some good reason. The history of the main trophies and major competitions gives a picture of the gradual build-up to golf in the ladies' section as it is today.

TROPHIES

Graycroft Trophy/Challenge Trophy

This is one of the earliest competitions, although its origins are unknown. However, in 1923 it was "won outright by Mrs Bland". The committee therefore decided to buy a replacement and suggested that 40 ladies gave 5/- (25p) each. A silver trophy was purchased to be called the "Moortown Ladies' Challenge Trophy". It started as an aggregate of four medal rounds in two weeks but in 1963 this was changed to three rounds out of four to count, and since 1977 has been drawn and played as two medal rounds in the same week.

Golf Medal/Annual Medal

This was also one of the earliest major competitions and started in 1912. It was called Gold Medal Day and was played over 36 holes with a draw for partners and presentation of a medal. In 1925 it was decided to have a second class Gold Medal also. Later on it was played as a finals day for all those who had won monthly medals during the previous twelve months. In 1996 two silver salvers were purchased from Miss Cecile Anderson's bequest for the winners in the Silver and Bronze divisions.

Ryder Cup

This has always been a qualifying round with a 30 handicap limit followed by match play for the top eight (formerly 16). Until the 1939–45 war a 36-hole final was played. At the A.G.M. in 1979 Mrs Sandbach was asked to present the Ryder Cup to the winner on its 50th anniversary as she had done when Captain on the first occasion. In 1989 the then Lady Captain, Miss Sheila Yeadon, and that year's winner, Miss Elizabeth Speak appeared on the local I.T.V. Calendar programme to show viewers the Cup and explain its history. The Lady Captain, Mrs Rita Shaw, and winner, Mrs Linda Hudson (now Fell), were on the same programme again in

The Ladies own Ryder Cup

2004, the year Europe managed to win the 'other' Ryder Cup! The original Cup is now considered so valuable that it is no longer in the ladies' trophy cupboard but resides in a vault. A replica can be seen in the trophy cupboard.

Coronation Cup

In 1937 a Mrs Johnson presented a trophy to be known as the Coronation Cup to celebrate the Coronation of King George VI. It was decided that this should be a qualifying round followed by match play for the top eight but in 1969 the format was changed to a popular one round foursome stroke competition.

J Arthur Sykes Salver

In 1956 the new President gave a silver salver to the ladies. This is played as a qualifying round competition followed by match play for the top eight qualifiers. In 1958 he decided that this should be won outright and a larger salver was presented in its place.

Jubilee Trophy

Miss Elsie Greenwood presented this magnificent silver engraved tray to the ladies in 1959 to commemorate her "50 years of happy membership at Moortown", together with an endowment. In that year also she was made an Honorary Life member, and in recognition of the event this friendly and popular member, who had been Treasurer for 11 years, was presented with a silver ash tray.

Jeken Trophy

In 1956 Mr Jeken offered a silver cup to the ladies to be played for in memory of his mother. It was decided that this should be called the "Alice Jeken Cup" and would be for members over 50 years of age to be played for over one round.

Lupton Trophy

In 1972 the nieces of Miss Betty Lupton, left a bequest in her memory for the purchase of a trophy to be played for annually. A silver dish was chosen for a 'round robin' tournament but in 1975 it was decided that this should be a drawn winter knock-out.

A collection of the 2008 Ladies Trophies on the new Centenary Table Cloth

Scratch Trophy
In 1990 Miss Beryl Pickering presented a trophy for a best gross competition to be played for annually over 36 holes in one day.

Betty Lodge Trophy
This was given to the ladies in 1991 by Betty Lodge's daughter in memory of her mother — a past Captain and pre-war member. It was decided to make this a Bronze Division competition with an 18-hole qualifying round and a match-play knock-out for the four top qualifiers.

Mollie Thompson Trophy
Mrs Marjorie Hudson, gave a cut glass bowl to the Club in the memory of Mollie Thomson in 2000, and it was decided that this would be a 13-hole Stableford competition for the over 65s to be played for annually.

Penuel Laws Salver
This was given by Eric Laws in 2004 in memory of his wife who had been Lady Captain and Secretary. As Penuel disliked medals it was decided that the competition should be a Stableford for Silver Division players only.

Rosemary Readman Trophy
This attractive figure of a lady golfer was given to the ladies in 2008 in memory of Rosemary by her husband to be played as a par competition over 18 holes.

Hole-in-one Salver
In 1995 a silver salver was given to the ladies by Mrs Mollie Thompson. It had belonged to Betty Lodge — her late sister — and it was decided to use it to record any hole-in-one achieved by members.

Two Silver Cups
In 1998 Mrs Joan Baldwin gave two silver cups to be awarded to annual Stableford winners in Silver and Bronze divisions.

Reduction Cups
Miss Gladys Winn gave two small silver cups to the ladies in 1962. These were presented to the players in the Silver and Bronze divisions who had reduced their handicaps the most during the year.

Mrs Sharman's Trophy

Mrs Irene Sharman gave a small trophy in 1988, a golfer and ash tray and this is presented annually to the player with the four best monthly Stableford scores in the year.

Christmas Competition

This was played for the first time in December 1981 and has continued to the present day with no fixed format. Seasonal prizes are presented, funded from the competition entry fee.

Captain's Prize

This is not only the major competition of the year apart from the main trophies but is the earliest recorded competition to be shown on the Honours Board, starting in 1910. Originally the Captain's Day was a final, generally in the autumn, and the prizes to the winner and runner-up were given after the match. This was the culmination of a qualifying round with 16 to qualify, followed by knock-out rounds through the summer. Lady members would follow the final on the course before coming in for tea. This continued to be the format until at least 1959. The competition on Captain's Day is now a one round event followed by an enjoyable supper and prize presentation. A happy tradition decrees that the Lady Captain provides strawberries and cream to all present.

President's Prize

In 1970 the President, Mr R B Hopkins, offered a prize to be played for during the year. This set a precedent and there has been a President's Prize ever since, the format generally chosen by the ladies.

Lady Captain's Day July 2008
Lady Captain Caroline Learoyd, with former Lady Captains Anita Riley, Maureen Pitchford, and Jean Burrows

L.G.U. Medals and Stablefords

The monthly Medals and Stablefords have been played from the very early days and even continued throughout the 1939-45 war when all the other main competitions were in abeyance. Silver and subsequently plated spoons were given to the Medal winners, but from 1964 onwards the 'Bogey Competion' have been played as 'Stablefords', which members believe reflects more favourably on their golf with an occasional Par competition is held in the summer.

All Prize Day

Since before the 1939-45 war there has been an All Prize Day in the spring which launches the golf season when members bring a prize of designated value and after playing choose one from the prize table in order of merit.

Eclectic Competition

In 1933 a competition was introduced where a member could enter on cards kept in the locker room a particularly good score at any hole during the year if they played 18 holes, not necessarily in a competition. The format has now changed and the computer summarises good scores in competitions only. Prizes are given in the Silver and Bronze divisions at the year end.

Captain v Secretary

This is a long established autumn fixture of which there is a reference in October 1921, and is intended as the closing competition of the golf season. The tradition was that the losing team paid for a tea after the match.

Open Meetings/Invitation Meetings

Open meetings were held regularly until 1952 and were most successful financially, but then ceased and invitation meetings became the choice. Since 2002 there have been both open and invitation meetings.

Calvert Rose Bowl

A knock-out mixed foursomes competition has been played each year since the early 1960s, and from 1970 an Honours Board in the entrance hall recorded the winners. In 1991 Margaret Calvert received her Hon. Life membership and donated a silver rose bowl for presentation to the winners. It had been the Captain's Prize won by her father, James W Foreman, in 1939, and she was happy that this should finally have a permanent home at the Club.

The knock-out competition has in the past been very popular and the dinner in the autumn for the speeches and presentation of the prizes was one of the highlights of the year to the extent that only those who entered the competition and their husbands/wives were eligible to attend! In its heyday support reached 100 despite this restriction.

Outside Competitions

The Yorkshire Ladies' County Golf Association was founded in 1900 and its first President was Her Grace the Duchess of Devonshire. It has grown over the years into a highly successful and thriving association of some 146 Yorkshire Clubs. The Inter-Club matches are, of course, an important County feature, but there are various other competitions during the year including spring and autumn meetings. The main trophies played for each year, however, are as follows:-

Championship Trophy — This has been played since 1902 and is the premier Yorkshire trophy. It consists of a 36-hole qualifying competition followed by knock-out played off scratch, and only the low handicap golfers enter. Moortown's best players enter each year, and we have often had a qualifier but so far no actual winner.

Yorkshire Challenge Bowl — The first Challenge Bowl was held as early as 1901 with a qualifying round followed by a knock-out for the top 16, played off handicap. Success was elusive for Moortown for many years, but in 1975 Miss Louise Robson, who was only 17 at the time, won the Bowl at Hull, followed by Mrs Jane Stephenson at Bradford in 1980, Mrs Julia Watson (now Hicks) at Otley in 2001 and Mrs Lynn Wallis at Woodsome Hall in 2004.

County Foursomes Trophy — This competition was introduced in 1948 with players qualified on their own course and then on to the District Finals, with approximately 120 Clubs now playing in the District Finals. Moortown has been successful on only one occasion, the winners being Mrs Pat Wainman and Mrs Paddy Pullan in 1977.

THE YORKSHIRE LADIES' VETERANS GOLF ASSOCIATION

The YLVGA was formed in 1932 in association with the main Y.L.C.G.A., but with its own Captain, Committee and competitions. Many of our members have participated in the various events over the years. "Veterans" have to be 50 or over and the fact that competitions are now frequently oversubscribed gives credence to a remark at the very first A.G.M that *"one's power of enjoyment does not lessen with increasing years"*.

Championship Trophy — Mrs Carol Atack and Mrs Rosemary Readman have been successful in this competition.

Veterans' Foursomes Trophy — This Medal competition dates from 1973 and our winners have been Mrs Sheila Hardy and Miss Cecile Anderson in both 1977 and 1978, and Mrs Joy Brown and Mrs Margaret Calvert in 1989.

Handicap Trophy — This was given in 1951 and Moortown has been successful on four occasions to date, by Mrs Maisie Robson in 1963, Mrs Sheila Hardy in 1976, Mrs Mary Clarke in 1980 and Mrs Jean Burrows in 1982.

Garforth Team Trophy

This is an annual event held at Garforth for a Scratch and Handicap team of four, and Moortown has entered two teams each year. The Handicap Trophy dates from 1938 and our team has won in 2000 and 2005. The Scratch Trophy was given in 1950 and we have been successful in 1950, 1984, 1986–95, 2001, 2003 and 2004.

Leeds and District Winter Alliance

In 1966 this Alliance was formed and most Leeds Clubs took part with foursomes in the six winter months at fixed venues. Points were given for the best cards returned and a salver was presented at the end of the winter to the Club with the most points. Moortown did remarkably well and after six years had won the salver four times and been runners-up twice. In 1992 it was decided that the Alliance had become too large (20 Clubs), and a breakaway Alliance was formed of ten North Leeds Clubs. This has proved more manageable and four meetings are held over the winter months. After a few unsuccessful years Moortown has won the trophy in 2002/3, 2004/5 and 2007/8.

Alternative Day Players (A.D.P.)

This team competition was launched by the Y.L.C.G.A. in 2001 to allow those golfers unable to play during the week to take part in matches at weekends. A team comprises three players, and 18-hole matches are played against three clubs, home and away. The top four qualifiers play a semi-final and final.

TEAM MATCHES

Inter-club matches were played from the very early days and there is a reference in the County minutes to a Match Secretary in 1921, but no County records were available until 1927. However, Moortown must have participated in matches practically from the start as the Club minutes in 1911 mention that "a grant of 10/6 per match be made to the ladies for five home matches", and in 1920 it was also mentioned that visitors' meals would be paid for by the Club.

In 1927 the County records show that there were Divisions 1 and 2, and teams played three matches, home and away, choosing their opponents. The four Clubs with the highest number of points played on a finals day for a Shield. The matches in both Divisions were played level and not off handicap.

In 1928 a system of recording results of inter-club matches was introduced, and in that year Moortown purchased a handsome bound book to contain the results of all matches. These record books (there are now three) trace the successes and failures of every member and every team from then onwards, and they make interesting reading.

The Captains' candid remarks in the books are sometimes illuminating, especially as to the conditions some matches encountered over the years. Nothing changes — fog, thunderstorms, heatwaves, blizzards, bitter cold, howling gales — trolleys blown over, and matches postponed due to flooding!

In 1936 when Moortown reached the finals day at Alwoodley there was a touch of class as the Princess Royal and Princess Helena Victoria watched part of the match. In 1937 the Y.L.C.G.A. suggested two teams for inter-club matches, a first team playing off scratch and second team as handicap, and to play for two new trophies. In 1958 a thirds team was introduced for bronze division players to be known as Handicap 'B'.

The method of clubs arranging their own matches was very satisfactory for a prestigious club like Moortown, and Captains preferred fixtures with a similar quality of course. The only problem was, that the clubs we played seemed on the whole to have much stronger teams and our results reflected this, particularly when the matches were played level. In 1971, it was decided that the scratch teams should be drawn, and in 1976 this applied equally to the Handicap teams.

As with all major competitions, no inter-club matches were played during the war. They restarted in 1947 but, for several years, not only was petrol rationing in operation, but few members had cars, and the sheer practical difficulties of playing away matches meant that clubs made fixtures as local as possible. Fortunately this was long before matches were drawn by the County.

In 1928 our Committee decided to introduce ties for team members to be worn by present and past team players who had played in three matches — these to be "plain with a monogram at the end". There is no further mention of ties, but in 1960 specially made enamel brooches for the Captain and team members were purchased — the team brooches to be worn during the matches only and then handed in. In 1983

1960 A Team v Cobble Hall
Left to Right - Edna Millar, Lily Booth, Kath Graham, Margaret Foreman (now Calvert), Mary Eley, Mrs McKay, Cecile Anderson, Min Green

1970 A Team Finalists
Olga Parker, Joan Baldwin, Vi Marwood, Pat Wainman, Margaret Calvert, Mary Clark, Cecile Anderson

1989 B Team Winners
Ann Spencer, Sue Hillam, Sheila Yeadon, (l-r standing)
Maureen Pitchford, Irene Smith, Anne Gaines and Margaret Calvert (l-r seated)

team sweaters were suggested and have been worn by players ever since, colours being changed periodically. In 2003 brooches were proposed for each of the three teams and the following year they were in use.

It may not always be appreciated how difficult it is for teams to qualify for finals day. In fact, in 1930 in an attempt to improve standards it was decided that the team should meet every week for a practice session. It was not until three years later, however, that the team reached the semi-finals. At present there are 40 Scratch teams, 109 Handicap "A" teams and 127 "B" teams. It is usually necessary for teams to win all their matches, or perhaps halve one match, to qualify for the finals day, playing a semi-final in the morning and, if fortunate to win, playing a final in the afternoon. There is naturally great excitement when one of our teams does qualify.

Scratch Team

From 1966 when Moortown first entered a Scratch team we have reached finals day seven times, qualifying for the actual final in the afternoon three times, but failing to win the trophy.

Handicap "A" Team (Scratch – 25)

This team first reached finals day in 1933 but failed to take the trophy, and in all we have achieved the final 11 times, taking the trophy four times, in 1947, 1951, 1973 and 1980.

Handicap "B" Team (19 – 36)

We first entered a "B" team in 1970, and have reached finals day eight times, winning the trophy three times, in 1971, 1979 and 1989.

Small brass shields are given to clubs winning the semi-finals and finals, and our successes can be seen displayed on the Welsh dresser in the ladies' lounge. Achievements have eluded the Club over recent years — but we keep trying.

Footnote

In 2006 the record in these team matches of the four present Hon. Life members is worth a mention, if only to show the outstanding support they have given to the Club over the years, this despite full-time careers and other responsibilities. Mrs Sheila Hardy has played in 119 matches, Mrs Margaret Calvert in 190, Mrs Joan Whitehurst in 77 and Dr Isobel Alexander in 78. The first three have played in all divisions, Scratch, 'A' and 'B', as their golf has fluctuated, and Isobel in the Scratch and 'A'.

Evening League

This is a Leeds and District League which at present consists of seven local clubs, and has been running since 1995. It is a 9-hole singles match play competition for teams of five with its own special scoring system. Moortown joined in 1999 and won the trophy in 1999, 2003, 2004, 2005, 2006 and 2007.

Social Activities

From the early days the ladies played a very active role in social events at the Club. They organised whist drives, provided refreshments and served on the House Committee, for which the Club committee records many votes of thanks to the ladies. Bridge became the favoured card game by 1921 and afternoon and evening mixed bridge drives were held regularly during the winter months. They organised a

1998 Scratch Team finalists at Ganton
Alison Mowat, Kay Baxter,
Rosemary Redman, Dorothy Glass,
Carol Atack, Didi Powers, Sally Best Captain, Janice Kerr

2006 Winners of Huddersfield Salver
Julia Hicks, Ailsa Jarvis, Beverley Burrows, June Smethills,
Lynn Wallis Maire McCarthy, Jane Slinger, Glenys Smart,
Rita Shaw, Angie Gault, Dianne Thompson

2008 North Leeds Alliance
Alma Rostron, Linda Hudson, Rita Shaw, Cheryl Hill,
Lady Captain Liz Boldy, Carol Atack, Vicky Renny,
June Smethills, Maire McCarthy, Julie Ballantyne,
Marianne Cooke, Margaret Allen, Marlene Roberts,

gymkhana in 1926 towards funds which was highly successful and raised £189. An entertainment committee was formed, and the ladies appeared to organise and sell tickets for the Club dances which were held monthly in the winter until 1939, and in 1931 even did the catering. These dances usually made a profit for the ladies' funds, but in 1935 it was recorded that profits should go to the Club funds in future. Children's Christmas parties were also organised by the ladies.

Mixed bridge was held monthly in the evenings in the 1960s but folded in 1971, to be reinstated in 1982. since then interest has been sporadic, but duplicate bridge has now become popular and since 2002 there has been some interest in mixed bridge sessions in the winter.

In 2003 a large charity bridge drive for the Martin House Hospice was hosted by the ladies and has since been held each winter with great success, raising a large amount of money.

Rubber bridge has been played on most golf days all the year round by non-golfers or after golf. The minutes record references in past years to complaints about "selfish people" refusing to give way when others were waiting for a game. Various suggestions were made to solve the problem, but in the end it was left to the ladies themselves to sort out. They decided on a 'half-hour rule', after which there would be 'cutting out'. Since 1947 there is silence so natural courtesy must have prevailed.

In 1936 a 'ping-pong' table was given to the Club and was situated in the present TV lounge. It was very popular for a time with a sub-committee formed to run tournaments, but interest dwindled and the table was given away to a W.A.A.F. station in Headingley during the war.

In 1953 a ladies' luncheon club was formed, and the first luncheon was held in the January. The guest speaker was the men's Captain, Mr C Atkinson, who recited a poem by Lord Alfred Tennyson. This rather uplifting subject matter would appear to have set a high standard for the luncheons, and he was followed by the Editor of the Yorkshire Post, a Contract Bridge expert, a Constance Spry flower arranger, and Wimbledon tennis player amongst others. The luncheons were held monthly during the winter with the Captain organising the speakers. After three years, however, the difficulty of finding so many suitable speakers brought the venture to a close.

In 1977 the Captain, Miss Elizabeth Speak, suggested a New Year luncheon, which was successful, and in 1981 Mrs Ellen Brown, who was then Captain introduced a speaker as in the 1950s. This function has continued each winter ever since, and the speakers, arranged by the Captain, have lectured on a great variety of subjects. A visitors book records their names and specialities.

A Christmas lunch was suggested in 2000 preceded by a 'fun' 9-hole competition. This has become an annual event which is enjoyed and well supported.

In 2008 the Centenary Captain-elect decided to organize equipping the ladies with Edwardian Golf costumes for the forthcoming centenary events. In the absence of any ready made costumes she settled on sourcing some suitable material from the United States and set about the job of making the costumes together with fellow lady members. The ladies lounge was turned into a sewing room and the resultant outfits as seen at the beginning of the chapter were unfurled at the Gibraltar Day in September at the start of the centenary celebrations.

PERSONALITIES AND SPECIAL ACHIEVEMENTS
Honorary Members

These awards are made only rarely to those who have given special service to the Club during their years of membership. They are distinct from ladies who have been members for 50 years continuously, when Honorary Life Membership is automatically granted.

Mrs Bland — was one of the original members and was the first Captain in 1910. she appears from the Honours Board to have been Captain also in 1912, 1920 and 1927. She was Captain of Yorkshire in 1925 and also played in the Yorkshire County Team matches from 1920–1927 (8 years running). In addition she played top of the Moortown team in inter-club matches "cheerfully and successfully for 25 years", for which a small acknowledgement was presented to her at the A.G.M. in 1934. She was awarded Honorary Membership by the Club in 1937.

Miss Pollard — was also one of the original members and was in office as Secretary from 1916–1936. In 1926 she was elected an Honorary Member for her services and in 1931 was presented with a platinum and diamond wrist watch from the ladies for all her work. She also received a "large bunch of roses from the Captain, Secretary and Treasurer of the men's section". In office she was a formidable character by all accounts; but Margaret Calvert only remembers her as a gentle old lady living with her niece, Mrs Sandbach, and always wearing rather beautiful and elaborate feathered hats. She died in 1964 aged 93.

Mrs Davies — was granted Honorary Membership in 1951. She had then been a member for 40 years and a much respected Secretary for 15 years, 11 of them as joint Secretary/Treasurer with Miss Greenwood. On her resignation in 1951, when she left Leeds, she was presented with a Rolex watch and leather handbag.

Mrs Emmie Walkland — as is commemorated elsewhere in the ladies' section, her record is unique in services to the club. She joined Moortown in 1929, and was Captain from 1938–1945 during all the war years when, apart from her other duties, she endeavoured to keep interest in golf alive in the section to provide some light relief for the members. She gave a Captain's Prize each year of the war. On relinquishing office in November 1945, she was presented with a tea trolley and cheque to mark the esteem and appreciation of her seven years' captaincy. She was Hon. Treasurer from 1946–1951, and then Hon. Secretary from 1952–1978. In 1972 the Club awarded her Honorary Membership. She gave the annual Eclectic prizes from 1951–1981, also working out the results from the entries. After this she was always on duty checking competition cards at the Invitation meetings until 1986. She had also been Hon. Secretary of the Yorkshire Ladies' Veterans for 16 years. She died in 1990, aged 97.

Mrs Butler — was invited to be an Honorary Member of the Club by the Chairman in 1957 for her services to Moortown.

HONORARY LIFE MEMBERS

1959	Miss Elsie Greenwood
1963	Mrs Baxter, Mrs Sandbach
1969	Mrs Gash
1987	Mrs Irene Sharman
1991	Miss Cecile Anderson, Mrs Margaret Calvert
1992	Mrs Fionnguala McCarthy
2000	Mrs Sheila Hardy
2005	Mrs Joan Whitehurst
2006	Dr Isobel Alexander

The Ladies Sewing Club preparing for the centenary

Emmie Walkland's 90th Birthday Party
Margaret Calvert, Irene Sharman, Maureen Pitchford, Norma Burton, Emma Walkland, Captain Joan Barrett, Joy Brown, Isobel Alexander, Joyce Forster, Pauline Thorpe, Joan Baldwin, Olga Parker

Rosemary Readman

MEMBERS SPECIAL ACHIEVEMENTS

Mrs Rosemary Readman — was Captain in 1994, when she also won the Yorkshire Veterans' Championship. She had a handicap of +2 in 1979 and in the July Medal 1981 scored a gross 66, which was a course record. As the course was altered in 1989 this achievement stands permanently. At one time she had the third lowest handicap in England. Tragically, Rosemary was killed when she was hit by a vehicle whilst on holiday with her family in Tenerife in April 2007, aged 67.

Mrs Vi Marwood — joined Moortown in 1947 and played for the County in 1952. She was Captain in 1968 and served as President of the Y.L.C.G.A. from 1970–72. In 1962 she was Captain of the Yorkshire Veterans.

Rosemary's card

Mrs Sheila Hardy — joined in 1950 and, with a handicap of 3, played for the Yorkshire County in several matches between 1959 and 1963, and also for the Yorkshire Veterans in 1973 and 1974.

Dr Isobel Alexander — has been a member since 1956 and Captain twice, in 1969 and again in 1990. With a handicap of 3 she played in the Yorkshire County team in 1968 and 1969. In 1978 and 1979 she played for both the Yorkshire Veterans and the Northern Veterans.

Mrs Jean Burrows — was Captain in 1973. She acted as Competition Secretary for the Y.L.C.G.A. for 14 years and in 1990 served as Captain of the County.

Mrs Mary Clarke — was Captain in 1970 and acted as Hon. Secretary of the ladies' section from 1990–1993. She became Hon. Secretary of the Y.L.C.G.A. in 1979, serving 10 years in that capacity, and was Captain of the County in 1980. She was also Captain of the Yorkshire Veterans in 1994.

Mrs Carol Atack — joined Moortown in 1985. She was Yorkshire Veterans' Champion in 1988, 1989, 1990, 1992 and 1995, and was Captain of the Yorkshire Veterans in 2001. In 1989, 1991 and 1994 she was Northern Veterans' Champion. As a member of the English Senior Ladies' Association she was a team member in the European Senior Ladies' Team Championship in 1990 and 2000, when on both occasions England were the winners. She was Captain of this Association for two years, 2001–2003.

Carol Atack

LADY CAPTAINS

Year	Name	Year	Name	Year	Name
1910	Mrs Bland	1950	Mrs G Green	1981	Mrs R H Brown
1911	Mrs Metcalf	1951	Mrs A B Sharman	1982	Mrs J I M Pitchford
1912	Mrs Bland	1952	Mrs W H McMinn	1983	Mrs J Barrett
1913	Mrs Pegler	1953	Mrs R C Cartwright	1984	Mrs K Burton
1914	Mrs Butler	1954	Mrs H Graham	1985	Mrs M J Riley
1915	Mrs Baxter	1955	Mrs A E H Maughan	1986	Mrs R J Parker
1916–18	Mrs Craven	1956	Mrs R C Southcott	1987	Mrs R J Smith
1919	Mrs Butler	1957	Mrs A B Sharman	1988	Mrs R G Sinclair
1920	Mrs Bland	1958	Mrs J W Kidd	1989	Miss S M Yeadon
1921	Mrs Wilkinson	1959	Mrs G Eley	1990	Dr I B Alexander
1922	Mrs Drake	1960	Mrs M Green	1991	Mrs M A Spencer
1923	Mrs Kellett	1961	Mrs R Learmonth	1992	Mrs B Bertrand
1924–25	Mrs Stembridge	1962	Miss M V Foreman	1993	Mrs C G Hill
1926	Mrs Metcalf	1963	Mrs E Wilson	1994	Mrs R Readman
1927	Mrs Bland	1964	Mrs H G Graham	1995	Mrs L E Hudson
1928	Mrs Green	1965	Miss C Anderson	1996	Mrs A J Jarvis
1929	Mrs Knight	1966	Miss J Forster	1997	Mrs A Rostron
1930	Mrs Sandbach	1967	Mrs A E H Maughan	1998	Mrs S E Best
1931	Mrs Lawson-Brown	1968	Mrs G Marwood	1999	Mrs J Whitehurst
1932	Mrs J F White	1969	Dr I B Alexander	2000	Mrs P A Laws
1933	Mrs J S Logan	1970	Mrs B H J Thompson	2001	Mrs L Wallis
1934	Mrs H Wyndham-West	1971	Mrs G F Lodge	2002	Mrs S Winn
1935	Miss M C Green	1972	Mrs K M Baldwin	2003	Mrs M P Cooke
1936	Miss E Greenwood	1973	Mrs J R Burrows	2004	Mrs R Shaw
1937	Mrs Butler	1974	Mrs T B Foster	2005	Miss M S McCarthy
1938	Mrs T V Kean	1975	Mrs M Plows	2006	Mrs J R Slinger
1939-45	Mrs E Walkland	1976	Mrs J Brown	2007	Mrs R M Cooke
1946	Mrs Smithson	1977	Mrs F Burrow	2008	Miss C Learoyd
1947	Mrs W H McMinn	1978	Miss J E Speak	2009	Miss A W Allen
1948	Mrs G Eley	1979	Mrs E N Pullan		
1949	Mrs R B Graham	1980	Mrs E M Thompson		

LADY SECRETARIES

1916 – 1936	Miss Pollard
1937 – 1947	Mrs Davies and Mrs Greenwood (Joint Secretary and Treasurer)
1947 – 1951	Mrs Davies
1952 – 1979	Mrs E Walkland
1987 – 1990	Mrs J Brown
1991 – 1993	Mrs M Clarke
1994 – 1996	Mrs D Glass
1997 – 1999	Mrs P Laws
2000 – 2001	Mrs S Winn
2001 – 2003	Mrs S Best
2004 – 2006	Mrs L Wallis
2006 – present	Mrs A Jarvis

Ladies Captain's Day 2008, left to right: Susan Harley, Lady Captain Caroline Learoyd, Jane Slinger

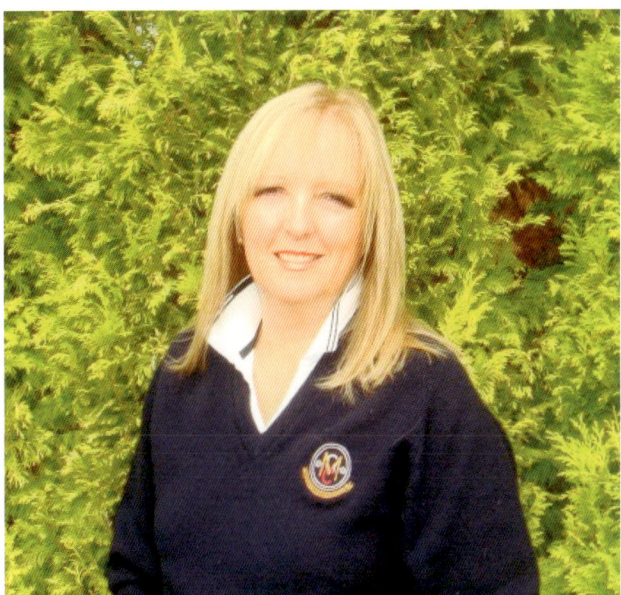

Centenary Lady Captain Adele Allan

Tom Watson playing with Victor Watson and Don Revie in the 1976 Watsons v The Rest of the World

XIV VISITORS AND VISITS

TOM WATSON

Moortown's standing as a major championship venue has attracted many visitors to the club, from the best-known professionals to keen amateurs and club golfers alike. But, in the distinguished annals of Moortown, few visits have been more unusual than that engineered by one of the club's elder statesmen, Victor Watson. In the summer of 1976, the year of his captaincy, he devised an ambitious scheme: the Watsons versus the Rest of the World.

One of the Watsons he had in mind was his namesake, Tom Watson, who was duly invited to join Victor and some others - including Henry Cotton and Don Revie - to play Moortown with a different two at each hole. The event took place on July 2nd and is perhaps best described by its originator.

"My year as Captain of Moortown Golf Club was blessed with marvellous weather. It was a wet Winter and a damp Spring but when Summer began it went on and on, merging into a delightful Autumn. Early on I had wondered what to do to make it a memorable year and hit on the idea of inviting Tom Watson to come to play at Moortown. He had won the Open at Carnoustie in 1975, his first major tournament and virtually the start of his great career. But he was not at that time a super star. So when I tried to telephone him I got straight through to his home and spoke to his wife Linda. She told me that all Tom's business was

Victor and Tom Watson watching Peter Rogerson's drive on the old 6th Hole

Victor Watson and Don Revie watching Tom Watson drive

Tom Watson with Henry Cotton on the practice range

dealt with by her brother, a lawyer in downtown Kansas City. I phoned the lawyer and suggested that Tom and his wife should travel to the UK a day early on his visit to defend his Open title and take part in a special competition at Moortown the venue for the first Ryder Cup match in 1929. Tom agreed, a fee of $5,000 was agreed and all was set for a great day.

I was then managing director of John Waddington Ltd and made it a Company Day called The Watsons v The Rest of the World. Thirty-six players, mostly Waddington's customers were invited to play one hole each against Tom and I (off their handicaps, which took a bit of puzzling to make for a fair contest).

Tom and Linda stayed at the Post House at Bramhope and my wife and I had dinner with them soon after they arrived. They were delightful company and I was more than ever excited by the prospect of the next day which in the event dawned bright and warm. To add extra spice to the day I had invited Henry Cotton to come along and also the great Yorkshire amateur Alec Kyle. Just before lunch we had a short exhibition of shot making on the practice ground. Tom stunned us with his power and precision and then asked Henry to hit a few balls. The man who was once the world's best player took off his jacket, kept his ordinary walking shoes on and borrowed Tom's three wood. He placed a few balls on the ground and said "You see, your method depends on powerful legs, upper body strength and great arms. I could never hit the ball so far. I relied on the hands. But with the hands I could work the ball well. I could hit a straight shot" which he proceeded to do. "I could hook one or slice one" - he demonstrated both. "I could hit a low one or a high one" - and he produced examples of the two extremes. Tom said "I can't do that, and when I am your age I won't be able to play as well." Henry said "Yes, but you need to play as you do to win tournaments on today's golf-courses." He could have added - unless really bad weather intervenes in which case Henry's kind of skill comes into play.

We had a short lunch then all the players set off to practice their holes. The night before Tom had confided in me that the one thing he missed was being in the USA for the 4th July with all the fireworks which he loved. So I had got one of our livelier managers, Tony Murphy, to go to Standard Fireworks in Huddersfield to get some maroons of the type they use to gather the crews for the lifeboats. I thought we could start our competition with a bang. Tony found that they were out of maroons and bought Roman candles instead. It was a bad move which had a good result. One candle was let off, the gorse in front of the first tee caught fire, the fire brigade had to be sent for, consternation reigned and the Press had a field day with really good pictures in the next day's papers.

Eventually the first match got away, our opponents being Don Revie, the Leeds United manager and Derek Williamson a Waddington's sales manger who was such a good golfer

The oldest and youngest Players Willie Gaunt and James Robson take on the Watsons

Henry Cotton speaking at the Watson's Dinner with Victor, Tom Watson and Alex Kyle

Tom Watson speaking, watched by Victor Watson, Henry Cotton and Alex Kyle

that he wouldn't be put off by the occasion. Tom had no yardage chart, no knowledge of the course and was sometimes misled by advice from the crowd but he still managed a 66 and we won handsomely. But apart from the golf, what impressed the many members present was that I introduced Tom to two new men on each tee and he had remembered their names when the hole was over. Then in the evening he made an after-dinner speech which was eloquent and sincere in its praise for British courses and the ethos of golf in this country. Then we challenged all comers at snooker, and he turned out to be really good at that game too. So the Watsons had a field day. For all present it was a memorable occasion."

More recently, another distinguished visitor from the United States was the Mayor of New York, the legendary Rudolph Giuliani who became the focus of the world's attention and respect in the dark days of the 9/11 attack on the Twin Towers. The timing of his visit to Yorkshire enabled a photo call during which he performed the opening ceremony of the much revamped Professional's Shop.

Other famous visitors down the years have included Australian Cricket Test teams together with their English counterparts. Arranged by the Forty Club, these golfing 'tests' took place on the Sunday of the Headingley Test Matches. In their heyday, the Leeds United soccer team were regular visitors, and in 2007, the 1966 England World Cup football team held a reunion with a round of golf at Moortown.

Celebrities, too, have trodden the Moortown sward including the actors Dennis Waterman and Rula Lenska who were given lessons by the then Pro, Bryon Hutchinson while they were filming in the area. Ian Botham also called in to play with Martin Heggie.

Rula Lenska and Denis Waterman with Bryon Hutchinson

Rudolph Giuliani opening Martin Heggie's refurbished Pro Shop

1966 World Cup squad playing at Moortown with Martin Heggie

Martin Heggie with Ian Botham

WORCESTER COUNTRY CLUB

In July 2000 the Club received an invitation from Massachusetts, USA, to attend the Worcester Country Club's Centennial anniversary in October of that year. Worcester hosted the first Ryder Cup in 1927, and stands unique as being the only course in the United States to have hosted the Ryder Cup as well as both the Men's and Ladies' U. S. Opens in 1925 and 1960, respectively.

The Moortown Captain and Chairman attended the impressive celebrations in the company of Jim Awtry, the Chief Executive Officer of the PGA of America and Sandy Jones, his opposite number at the European PGA.

Louisville's Mayor Jerry Abramson holding the engraved salver presented by Moortown to the City of Louisville, 2008

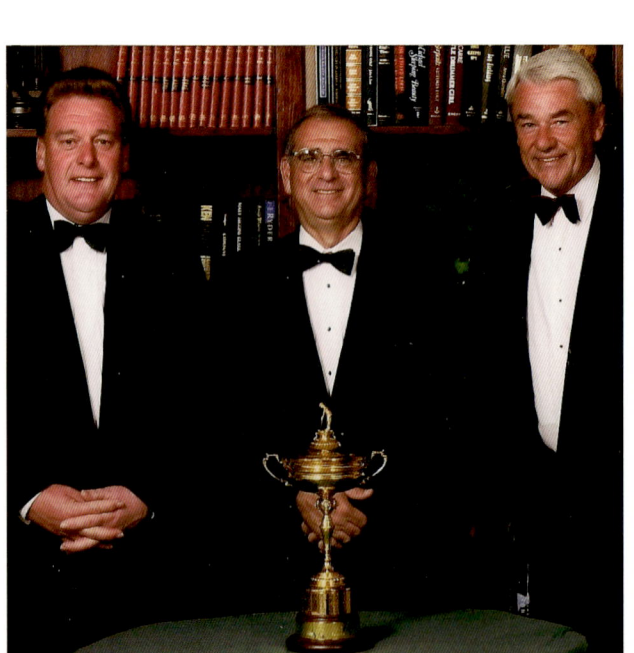

William J. Abodeely the President of Worcester Golf Club at their Centenary ceremony with Roger Eames Captain and Peter Rogerson Chairman of MGC with the Ryder Cup in Massachusetts, 2000

The Worcester Country Club clubhouse, the setting of their Centennial

VALHALLA, LOUISVILLE

A unique occasion took place in September 2008 during the Ryder Cup at Valhalla in Louisville, Kentucky. As Louisville was Leeds' sister city, a 5-strong official party from Moortown, representing the club and the city of Leeds, flew out as guests of Louisville's civic leaders, taking with them one of Moortown's most prized possessions, the replica of the original Ryder Cup, now known as the Ryder Commemoration Cup. Standing 13 inches tall on a 3 inch pedestal, the trophy was presented in 1929 by Sam Ryder to the ladies of Moortown in recognition of all the work they had done during the Ryder Cup.

Together with the club's collection of historic photos of the 1929 event which had been provided by Moortown, the cup was on display at the Louisville Visitors' Center throughout the competition – the first time that it had ever left Leeds.

The Ladies Ryder Cup on display at an event at Churchill Downs Steve Beshear, Governor of Kentucky is in the party and Stan Curtis, Chairman of the Mayor's Ryder Cup Task Force together with Moortown officials.

Security for the Ladies Ryder Cup in Louisville

Martin Heggie, Roger Eames, David Sheret, The Captain and his wife at the entrance to the Moortown Village hospitality area at Valhalla

Trophy Cabinet in the MacKenzie Smoke Room

XV CLUB TROPHIES AND CHAMPIONS

Competitive golf in the form of monthly medals and club competitions has been a feature of Moortown's golfing calendar since its foundation. A major function of the Golf Committee was to organise and run all these competitions and adjust handicaps accordingly.

One event on the Moortown golfing calendar between 1927 and 1951 was the Moortown Open Meeting held annually in the first week in September. The programme of events for this meeting was:

Thursday am	*Ladies stroke competition*
Thursday pm	*Ladies 4 ball bogey competition*
Friday am	*The Moortown Trophy qualifying round 18 holes by strokes. Handicap limit 5. First 8 qualify to play off by match play*
Friday pm	*The Moortown Trophy Round 1 Bogey Competition*
Saturday am	*The Moortown Trophy Semi-Finals Moortown Championship – 36 holes Medal Play from scratch*
Saturday pm	*The Moortown Trophy final Foursome bogey competition*

An additional 2 days were added to the programme from 1948 to allow a Boys' Tournament to be played. All the events were open to members of recognised golf clubs. In 1947 there were 86 entries for the Moortown Trophy, 24 of whom were Moortown members. The competitors' handicaps ranged from scratch to 12. The 8 best scores for qualifying ranged from 70 to 75 and H.N. Green from Oakdale Golf Club with a handicap of 8 and who qualified in 7th place was the winner of the trophy. The Open Meeting was very popular during this period and a source of revenue for the club. Cups were presented to the winners of the Moortown Trophy and the Boys' Championship. One wonders why the event was abandoned in the 1950s at a time when open events and invitation meetings were becoming increasingly popular. One wonders, too, whatever became of the two trophies?

MAJOR CLUB COMPETITIONS

The following competitions are classed as the major club competitions with trophies presented at the Annual Dinner.

Sydney Groves Foursomes

In 1952 the family of Sidney Grove presented the club with two silver tankards to be given annually to the winners of the Sidney Grove Foursomes Competition. Partners are selected by ballot, low and high handicaps paired together. The qualifying competition is 18 hole medal play with the first 8 qualifying for match play knock-out. The handicap limit was 20 with a stroke allowance of ½ the difference and all to be played off the yellow tees.

2005 Sydney Grove Foursomes winners
John Spencer and Derek Fieldhouse with Captain, Jeff Flint

Greenwood Shield

The Greenwood Shield, an 18 hole medal off white tees, was first presented in 1919. The first 16 qualifiers are seeded for matchplay off full handicap.

J Arthur Sykes Trophy

An 18 hole medal off white tees. The first 8 qualifiers are seeded for matchplay off full handicap

Scratch Cup

In 1939 B S Lister presented the Scratch Cup to be played for over 36 holes stroke play off the blue tees over two days in one weekend. Qualifying for handicap purposes but not counting for aggregate. The top 8 players qualify for Club Championship as below.

Club Championship

An 18 hole scratch match play knock out seeded from Scratch Cup, off blue tees.

2005 Greenwood Shield winner
Steve Boldy with Captain Jeff Flint

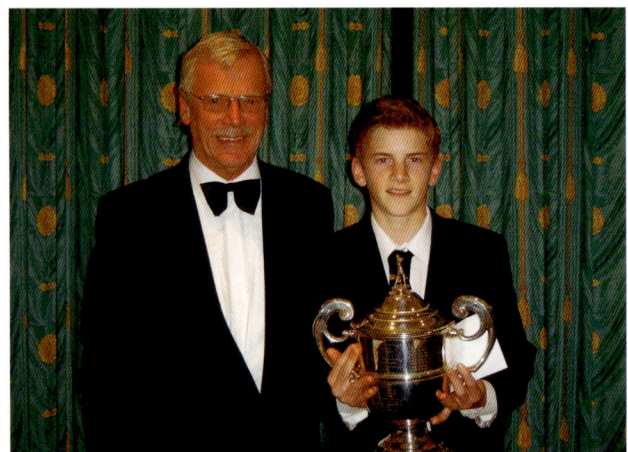

*Bradley Snowden receiving the 2005
J Arthur Sykes trophy from Geoff Flint*

Braime Trophy

In 1931 F Braime donated the Braime Trophy, an 18 hole medal competition off the white tees. Qualifying competition for handicap and aggregate with handicap limit of 20.

Veterans' Trophy

T and J C Bentley presented a Veterans' Cup in 1932 open to competitors aged 55 or over on the date of the competition.

*2005 Club Championship
winner Paul Snowden with Captain Jeff Flint*

It is an 18 hole medal competition off yellow tees. Qualifying competition for handicap and aggregate.

Hartley Trophy

Open to competitors aged 70 or over on the date of the competition which is an 18 hole medal off yellow tees. Qualifying competition for handicap and aggregate.

Freddie White Trophy

J F White, one of the club founders, died in 1937 and Moortown bought the Freddie White Cup in his memory. The competition is an 18 hole medal off white tees. Qualifying competition for handicap and aggregate with a handicap limit of 20.

Hutchinson Salver

Bryon Hutchinson presented the club with a silver salver at his Testimonial Golf Day to be known as the "Hutchinson Salver" to be played for annually in one of the Saturday 18 hole medal competitions played off white tees. Qualifying competition for handicap and aggregate with handicap limit of 20.

Lawson-Brown Cup

The earliest cup to be played for was the Lawson-Brown Cup which was donated in 1909. At that time it was held on a summer Saturday on a medal basis. Since then it has become the main match play knock-out competition open to all gentlemen members in the Club. It is played over 18 hole watch play from the white tees in all rounds. Full Handicap with handicap limit of 20.

Captain's Prize

Captain's prize day is another longstanding event. It dates back to 1909 and, at the Captain's discretion, it is played for on Captain's day. Qualifying for handicap only and winners added to the honours board.

*2005 Freddie White Trophy
winner Allan Easton with Captain Jeff Flint*

President's Prize

This also dates back to 1909 and is a competition at the President's discretion played for on President's Day.

The MacKenzie Trophy

A 4 ball better ball match play championship; choose partners, 18 hole match play better ball knock out; no handicap limit; ¾ stroke allowance taken from lowest handicap; off white tees.

*2005 Hutchinson Salver winner
Ian Stead with Captain Jeff Flint*

*2005 MacKenzie Trophy winners
Chris Metcalfe and Jonathan Flint with Captain Jeff Flint*

*2005, The R&A Trophy being presented to
Steven Roberts and Simon Stephens by Geoff Flint*

*2005 Captain Pro Challenge winners
Colin Gaines and Mike Cooper with Captain Jeff Flint*

Calvert Rose Bowl

A mixed foursome knockout; choose partners; 18 hole match play; handicap limit of 20 for men and 30 for ladies; stroke allowance ½ combined difference; yellow tees for men and red tees for ladies.

R & A Trophy

An 18 hole 4 ball better ball medal; white tees, ¾ handicap stroke allowance.

Jubilee Trophy

On Saturday 26th September 1959, the day after the Jubilee Dinner, members, who must have been a resilient breed, played for the Jubilee Trophy donated by the President J Arthur Sykes to commemorate Jubilee year. The competition took the form of a foursome stableford over eighteen holes with partnerships of gentlemen, ladies or mixed allowed. The trophy is permanently fixed in the entrance foyer with the list of subsequent winners appended to the honours board below; open to members aged 18 and over on the date of the competition; couples must be made up of one member and one guest; gentlemen off yellow tees and ladies off red; handicap limit 20 for gentlemen and 30 for ladies; ¾ stroke allowance.

Captain Pro Challenge

Traditionally the Captain and Professional have challenged any two members to play in an annual better ball matchplay contest. An original Moortown trophy, "The Bachelors Cup",

*1998, Jack Cooke, Roger Limbert receiving the
Captain Pro Challenge from captain, Mike Craven*

which is no longer contested, was presented back to Moortown by John Lawson-Brown and now the recipients of this trophy are the members who beat the Captain and Pro by the biggest margin.

Collinge Trophy

In 1971 J.A. (John) Collinge presented a tankard for the gentleman returning the lowest gross score in the Veterans' Prize. This is run in conjunction with a medal competition for competitors aged 55 or over on the date of competition; 18 hole medal; best gross score from the Yellow tees.

Aggregate Prize

In 1967 R.E. (Dickie) Robinson donated a silver plate to be presented annually to the Aggregate Prize Winner - the gentleman golfer recording the lowest five net scores in the following designated competitions: the monthly medals between April and October, the spring, autumn and extra medals, the Greenwood Shield, the J R Arthur Sykes Trophy, the Braime Trophy and the Freddie White Trophy on a net difference basis.

CLUB CHAMPIONS

Year	Champion	Year	Champion
1949	R.B. Lawrence	1980	R. Evans
1950	R. Cartwright	1981	I.J.A. Stephenson
1951	J.H Wales	1982	A.D. Hyde
1952	A. Turner	1983	J.R.F. Allison
1953	R. Cartwright	1984	J.R.F. Allison
1954	A.E. Booth	1985	I.J.A. Stephenson
1955	R. Cartwright	1986	S.M. Bottomley
1956	J.R. Newbold	1987	M. Illingworth
1957	J.R. Newbold	1988	M.H. Crossley
1958	F.H. Myers	1989	M.H. Crossley
1959	A.E. Booth	1990	I.J.A. Stephenson
1960	A.E. Booth	1991	M.T. Cooper
1961	A.E. Booth	1992	I. Hartley
1962	G.C. Robson	1993	C.N. Gaines
1963	J.R. Newbold	1994	M. Illingworth
1964	A. Turner	1995	R. Treweek
1965	A. Turner	1996	D. Mann
1966	J.A.B. Corscadden	1997	N.R. Sweet
1967	G.M. Shaw	1998	N.R. Sweet
1968	E.B. Robinson	1999	N.R. Sweet
1969	J.B. Bunney	2000	N.R. Sweet
1970	J.B. Bunney	2001	S. East
1971	A.E. Booth	2002	N.R. Sweet
1972	E.B. Robinson	2003	N.R. Sweet
1973	G.C. Robson	2004	S. East
1974	P.B. Allen	2005	P Snowden
1975	A.D. Hyde	2006	S East
1976	M. Pounds	2007	S East
1977	G.M. Hutchinson	2008	P Snowden
1978	C.C. Bowyer		
1979	I.J.A. Stephenson		

1952 England v France International at Royal St.Georges, Sandwich T.J.Shorrock, Sam Brough, Alan Turner, M.J.Pearson

Moortown has been blessed over the years with many exceptional golfers but space precludes the inclusion of all their successes and achievements. However, it would be remiss not to highlight one or two recent champions and a family of golfing excellence.

ALAN TURNER

It may come as a surprise to learn that it was not until 1953 that one of Moortown's many exceptional players won the Yorkshire Amateur Golf Championship. The honour went to Alan Turner who beat Sam Brough in the final at Ganton by 3 and 2. Later in the year the club marked the occasion with a celebration dinner. Alan was to bring further distinction to the club as an English International and as a member of the R & A Championship Committee meanwhile at Moortown his record of service included the chairmanship of Greens and the General Committee as well as the offices of Captain and President.

McCARTHY FAMILY

Members of the McCarthy family have left their mark on competitive golf at Moortown over the years. David represented England at Boys (Blairgowrie) and Youth (Downfield and Pannal) international level, and was a semi-finalist at the British Boys at Moortown. He made in the region of 50 appearances as a Yorkshire County player and was a member of several victorious Moortown teams in both the Yorkshire 1st Division and the Leeds Team Championships. Twice over he was the Leeds Open Champion (Scarcroft and Pontefract).

His prolific record also included winning the Hawksworth Trophy, the Cleveland Salver and – on three occasions – the Hudson Trophy at South Herts. He was also a two-time winner of the Crosby Beacon Trophy at West Lancs where he represented Moortown.

His elder son, Duncan, became a Yorkshire County player and was the St Andrews Boys Champion in 1997, the Auchterlonie Spoon Winner in 2007 and the winner of the Sheffield Plate in 2006. He was also a member of the winning Moortown team in the Yorkshire 1st Division Team Championships at Hornsea and the Beacon Trophy at West Lancs.

His other son, Nick McCarthy, represented England at the Boys' Home Internationals at Moray. Like his elder brother, he was a Yorkshire County player and twice won the English County finals with Yorkshire at senior level, at Royal Cinque Ports and Cleveland in 2006 and 2007. At Boys' level he won the English County finals with Yorkshire at Little Aston. In 2004 he was the Yorkshire under-16 champion and in 2006 was runner-up in the Scandinavian Amateur. His other achievements include membership of the England under-21 squad and victories in the Hawksworth Trophy (2008), the Cleveland Salver (2008), the Oakdale Acorn (2007) as well as 3rd place in the Lee Westwood Trophy in 2006 and 2007. His Moortown team membership victories include the Yorkshire 1st Division Team Championships at Hornsea and the Beacon Trophy at West Lancs.

STEPHEN EAST

Since joining Moortown in 1998 when he was the Leeds Open Champion, Stephen has won the club championship four times and amassed a large collection of trophies including the British Mid-Amateur Championship in 2001; the English Mid-Amateur Championship in 1998, 1999, and 2001; the Yorkshire foursomes in 2004 and 2006 and the Yorkshire Mid-Amateur championship in 1999 and 2000.

He was a member of the Moortown team which won the Yorkshire 1st Division team championship in 2007 and in 2003 achieved a record number of appearances for Yorkshire: 218. He was also in the English National Squad in 2001 and 2002.

NIGEL SWEET

Nigel, like Stephen, has a trophy cabinet full of silverware. He won the club championship six times from 1997. In Moortown's centenary year of 2009, he won the Yorkshire Amateur Championship at the third time of asking, defeating David Appleyard of South Leeds 4 and 3 in the final at Pannal. A former county amateur strokeplay champion, the matchplay title had eluded Nigel, who was beaten by Richard Law in the previous year's final and by Richard Finch in the 2001 decider.

Despite being fellow members of Moortown, Nigel Sweet and Stephen East, found themselves going head to head for the top honours in the 2009 European Mid-Amateur Championship at Rio Real Club in Marbella. It was an emotional duel with Nigel Sweet, who began the day as leader finishing second, just one shot from the champion; and with the Brazilian Rodrigo Lacerda, coming in third, two shots behind East. The winner scored a total of 217 shots, 1 over par.

Nick McCarthy England Boys International and Runner-Up Scandinavian U 21 Championship 2006

Stephen East with the 2001 British and English Mid-Amateur Champion Trophy

Nigel Sweet with the 2009 Yorkshire Amateur Trophy

Moortown Members embarking on one of their celebrated golf trips

XVI CLUB HAPPENINGS

GOLF TRIPS

Many a Moortown member has availed himself of a place on some celebrated golf trips, often organised by the professional and, in later years, by the club captain for the Captain's Awayday. Needless to say these functions are top rate sociable occasions, frequently necessitating coach travel from Moortown.

One such is worth recording. In 1983, the then pro, Bryon Hutchinson, organised a luxury Pullman-style coach to collect 40 members from Moortown and transport them in some style to The Open Championship at Birkdale. The club steward arranged for the caterer to supply a gourmet lunch to be served on board and Bryon used his influence to secure a spot not in the coach park but in the car park, which was close to the course and enabled the visitors to return to the coach at lunchtime. As luck would have it, many members of the Ilkley and Pannal clubs passed by the coach on their way to the course and were clearly envious of Moortown's de luxe arrangements. However, in the early evening of one of the warmest and driest days in the year, disaster struck when the Moortown coach attempted to turn round by the course fence. The coach's front wheels succeeded in submerging themselves in the sand below the grass. The same envious Ilkley and Pannal spectators, now on their way out of the course, found great amusement in watching the inebriated Moortown members attempting to push the coach, all to no avail. Two of the members joined J R Glover in abandoning ship and taking a taxi to John's father's house in Lytham; a difficult story to be relayed to the wives on being forced to stay in Lytham overnight.

THE SUGGESTION BOOK

Since its introduction in 1923 the Suggestion Book has become a Moortown institution without parallel. Kept in the Smoke Room, the purpose of the leather-bound volume is to allow full members a formal opportunity to acquaint the General Committee with the membership's views and concerns on the running of the club – some serious, some light-hearted. To that end, the Suggestions Book is placed on the table at every General Committee meeting whose members have had to ponder such weighty suggestions as:

"That seats be provided at all tees for the comfort of members making little progress on medal days."

In September 1961 one member ventured into controversial waters:

"It is suggested that as lady members of the club are not permitted to enter the smoking room except on very special occasions, no lady visitors should be allowed. Today at 5.15pm two are sitting in the window seats."

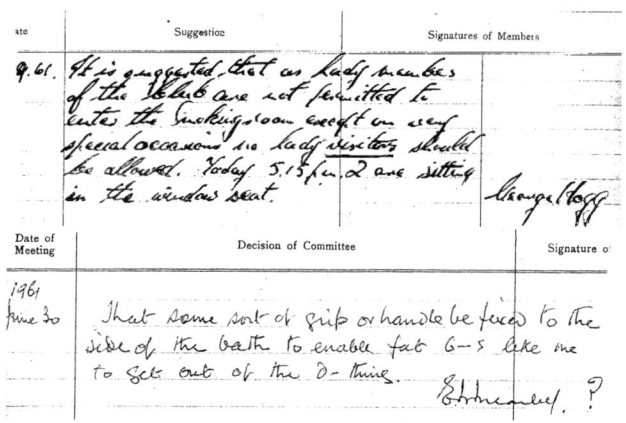

Taken from the Suggestion Book

In June of the same year another member shared a more personal problem:

"That some sort of grip or handle be fixed to the side of the bath to enable fat b*****s like me to get out of the b****y thing."

Clubhouse issues continued to fill the pages of The Suggestion Book down the years and in October of 1984 one writer vented his spleen on a relatively new-fangled issue:

"May I suggest: The fruit machine in the men's bar at the present time should be loaded upon an inexpensive mode of transport and swiftly taken many, many miles away, perhaps as an instrument of torture to be utilised by some such other unmentioned club as perhaps .... Moor Allerton, Alwoodley or, indeed, Tinshill Working Mens' Club."

However, the fruit machine was not without its friends, although five years later frustration was expressed at its mechanical efficiency:

"Now that we have at some expense the equivalent of the Best Room at the Gipton, can the committee apply its mind to fundamentals such as the electric supply system to the power points in the club. Gordon Wood and I were playing the fruit machine when on 3 occasions it went off, twice depriving us of winnings which had just registered. It also turns the till off – which cannot be good for business!"

In September of the same year one golfer thought it was high time that the committee considered an arithmetical issue which had arisen on the course:

"The new holes were opened in May, it is now September. Having just viewed the members' list there is no surname Einstein. Will you please replace the stroke index numbers in the tee boxes?"

Winter League La Manga with Past Captains Albert Geoffrey Parker, Michael Riley and Alan Day

Winter League La Manga with Donald Miller Hyde, Gerry Connolly, Mike Redwood and Manual Ballesteros

Midwood members clean up at Moortown - Bernard Brockhouse, the late George Fowler and Malcolm Arthurs, showing off their trophies: the Braime Trophy, the Greenwood Shield, The Sidney Groves and the Aggregate Prize.

Meanwhile back in the clubhouse in October 1994 :
"At the astronomical cost of 50p per day the club can acquire the Daily Telegraph and The Times, who knows the intellectual level of the club might improve from the input of knowledge acquired from these papers.
P.S. the majority of the members are not brain dead and would welcome papers with some substance."

The Committee, however, had a ready response:
"The committee cannot agree that the intellectual level of the club needs to be raised and cannot therefore support this request."

The provision of crisps in the bar was the subject of numerous entries over years, but the entreaties to provide them habitually fell on deaf ears. In January 1993, the proponents of crisps made a fresh onslaught, which was backed up by some serious research. They wrote:
"That potato crisps of a superior quality (perhaps "kettle chips") are made available at the Bar. To avoid appearing vulgar they could be served in bowls. Recent fact-finding missions to The Savoy (London) and The Carlton (Cannes) have proved crisp-positive, and only The Parkway (Leeds) disdains the crisp. We hope and trust you wish to keep company with the former rather than the latter'.

But the committee remained both unimpressed and unconvinced:
"It was agreed that crisps should not be made available at Moortown. This of course means that despite the very expensive research done by the signatories, we find the Parkway approach preferable."

CLUB GROUPS – BACHELORS' CLUB

Moortown, unlike many golf clubs, has never encouraged the formation of sections within the club, and it is surprising to find that a Bachelors' Club existed for a short time in the 1930s. They organised dances and held an annual golf tournament for the Moortown Bachelors' Trophy. Russell Cartwright was the winner in 1930 & 1931 and the last holder was J Lawson-Brown in 1934. His son, John, presented the cup to Moortown in 1989 as the trophy for the Captain-Professional Challenge.

CLUB GROUPS – WINTER LEAGUE

Two other groups of members who arranged their own friendly golf competitions are worthy of mention, "The Winter League" and "The Midwood Golf Society". The former was a winter Sunday morning competition comprising 16 members, each partnering each other with the resulting scores recorded in a league table. The eventual winner received the Winter League Silver Salver presented by the league President, usually wearing his Haig Whisky chain of office. Two presidents served with distinction and good humour; Albert Geoffrey Parker and Donald Miller Hyde. The Winter League survived for over 25 years with various members and numerous substitutes stepping in to cover the absences of

Billy Midwood

league members unable to play. Regrettably the Winter League has now run its course, though memories remain, particularly of the many golf trips which grew out of it, both day trips and more ambitious week-long expeditions to La Manga, Marbella, and Ireland.

CLUB GROUPS – THE MIDWOOD GOLF SOCIETY

In 1980 a popular and long-standing Moortown member, Billy Midwood, sadly passed away. But his golfing pals continued to play, just as they had with Billy, at 7.15 every Sunday morning, summer and winter, rain or shine. In 1982 Billy's widow, Mollie Midwood, donated £300 (not a sum to be sneezed at back in those days) to buy a trophy for which Billy's pals could compete. Thus the Midwood Cup was born, and with it the Billy Midwood Golf Society whose members played each week under the strict rules of one of its founder members, George Fowler. George sadly passed away within a couple of years so Billy's good friend, Arthur Rowell, then took up the reins. Arthur ran the society, with great success, for a further 20 years before retiring from active golf, although he's still to be found actively drinking in the clubhouse every Wednesday. Many of the original members, such as Matt White, the incorrigible Scottish vet, Dr Jack Rhodes, who kept Guinness in business and Jim (Bull) Thompson plus other later additions to the motley crew, such as Alf Alderson and Peter Hartley, have all left us to play on a more celestial golf course. The society has regularly donated to charity and was always open to any Moortown member who simply wanted to play golf in convivial company and many of the Midwood members joined that way, never having had the pleasure of meeting Billy.

In 1992, in order to pay tribute the man who was the real driving force behind the Midwood Society, another trophy was inaugurated — Wor Arthur's Pot — so named because of Arthur Rowell's origins in the far reaches of the North East. Since Arthur handed over the reins in 2003 the society plods on, a bit lost without him, but determined to play each year for the two pots and to keep alive the names of the two popular Moortown stalwarts in whose names they knock the ball around each week into unexplored parts of their wonderful golf course.

1969 HOW TO PLAY BETTER GOLF WITH JOHN JACOBS

In 1969 John Jacobs, one of the finest exponents of the game, set out in thirteen televised lessons a programme of instruction for the club golfer. John Jacobs had few equals and his lessons were therefore projected with authority and simplicity. John selected Moortown for this Yorkshire Television series featuring a panel of golfers, mainly Moortown members, as his pupils. The programmes were so successful that a second series of 13 was commissioned and as a result some of his pupils like Jean Burrows became recognisable TV stars. In the centenary celebrations of 2009 John Jacobs revisited the club and was re-united with some of his class of '69.

1974 BRABAZON TROPHY, CLUB HOUSE INCIDENT

The 19th was the location of a bizarre golfing incident which has now become part of Moortown's folklore. While playing in the 1974 English Open Amateur Stroke Play Championship, Nigel Denham, a member, played the 18th from the 19th, having hit his approach shot into the middle

John Jacob's Play Better Golf Book taken from the ITV Series

of the Smoke Room. At that time the clubhouse was not out of bounds and, although Nigel was entitled to a free drop from an immovable obstruction, he was not to know the rules and elected to play his ball, with the encouragement of the regulars in the bar. His resultant chip through a small open window finished six feet from the hole - a remarkable shot - but the story did not have a happy ending for the putt for a par four was missed. There was controversy later for, it was a summer's day and some of the windows were open, though the one the ball was played through was not - one of the regulars having opened it for Nigel. It was suggested that he should have been penalised for improving line of sight but nothing was said at the time and his score of 74 was allowed to stand. Needless to say, Nigel was careful to observe the clubhouse rule in force at that time and removed his spikes before entering the clubhouse to play his famous shot.

Nigel Denholme recreating his famous shot

Saucy Moortown Scorecard

1976 THE SAUCY MOORTOWN SCORE CARDS

In the same year of Victor Watson's captainship, Moortown had an unexpected stroke of luck. The so-called Mini-Ryder Cup was to be played at Hollinwell. between club professionals of the USA and the UK & Ireland. However, Hollinwell had been badly affected by the very hot, dry summer and Moortown was asked to stage the event instead.

Just for fun, Victor had the idea of producing score cards illustrated with nudes. He spoke to the President, Frank Brown, and said *"You know all those American clubs have score cards with pictures on and ours are just words and numbers, very plain. What about having a special card with pictures on just for the Mini-Ryder Cup event?"* *"Good idea"* said the President. Victor then showed him the proofs of the 'card that's never torn up' bearing the nudes. The President coughed and spluttered for a while. *"Well of course"* he finally said *"Jolly good joke, no concern to me but what about the Ladies?"* *"Shall I ask Emmie?"* Victor said *"and if it's ok by her, then go ahead."* Frank Brown agreed, though somewhat cautiously. Victor knew that Emmie Walkland would agree. She was a great sport, one of Moortown's much loved characters. So Victor produced the cards as souvenirs for the visitors and anybody else who wanted them. They are now collectors' items!

February 1976
OPENING THE NEW MEN'S SHOWERS.

The large crowd which assembled for this unusual event were in for a big surprise when the Lady Captain Joy Brown, persuaded by Victor Watson, the captain, agreed to perform the opening ceremony of the new men's showers. Much to her amazement, when Joy cut the ribbon and opened the door, there were two of Moortown's great characters Billy Midwood and Tony Heap, both decked out in Victorian bathing costumes.

Billy Midwood and Tony Heap with Captain Victor Watson and Lady Captain Joy Brown

Albert Geoffrey Parker

Joan Whitehurst, David Stead, Gerry Connolly, Don McClennan, Allison Mowet, Albert Parker, Sam Brough and Brian Pedley at Albert's Captain's Day

Marco Pierre White

ALBERT GEOFFREY PARKER

If any Moortown member ever deserved to be described as a living legend, then surely that someone must be Albert Geoffrey Parker. Stories abound of this golfer and raconteur, now in his eighties but still larger than life. So it seems appropriate that this centenary volume should tip its hat in Albert's direction and record for posterity one of his own favourite tales.

It arose some years ago out of a trip to Estoril organised by Bryon Hutchinson. In those days it was the practice of the Portuguese caddies to walk down the fairway ahead of the play to spot where their golfers' balls had come to rest and, how should we put this, to improve the lie a little for those in trouble.

Bryon teed off first with a cracking drive down the fairway, as hard and long as it was accurate. Albert struck his hard, too - but into the trees where it ricocheted in every direction, bouncing from branch to branch before dropping into the rough. Not his finest shot.

A few minutes later when the golfers joined their caddies Bryon was astonished to see that Albert's ball lay nicely placed on the fairway a foot or two ahead of his own. His reaction was explosive and included rather more than a hint of suspicion that Albert's ball had been helped back onto the fairway. However, the caddy in question was innocence personified, explaining: "me no touchee, we outdrive Hutchie" – an explanation that has deservedly become part of Moortown's folklore

But Albert was to add yet another footnote to the club's history in his schooling of a young caddy destined to become one of Britain's original celebrity chefs.

MARCO PIERRE WHITE

In those days the young Marco Pierre White lived just five minutes walk from the course. "When I was eleven I thought I'd become a caddy, he said. Marco Pierre continued: "The highlight of that job was caddying for Gerald Robson on the day that he was made Captain in 1975, though my first job some eighteen months earlier was not as much fun."

"I'd arrived at eight on a Saturday morning and joined the other caddies who were hovering awaiting commissions. Ten minutes later Bryon Hutchinson, the professional, emerged through the doorway and asked, 'Who wants a job?' Strangely, I was the only one to raise my hand. And then I discovered why. That ten-past-eight golfer was a regular and he had the heaviest golf bag in the history of the sport. I lugged it around 18 holes, hunch backed and panting."

"Come the following Saturday, I knew not to put up my hand. None of us did. 'Right lad,' he said to me. 'You were good last week. You can do it again.'"

"My favourite client was a certain Mr Parker (Albert Geoffrey), who was often kind to me (with twenty pence tips), but he also swore and shouted a lot. He played with a man known only to me as the Doctor (Jack Rhodes) and, as I was always dashing off to find the balls, Mr Parker nicknamed me Hawk Eye. One morning he was about to tee off when he stopped mid-swing and shouted, 'Hawk Eye, have you got my beer?' I scurried away to find a barman though when I relocated Mr Parker on the third fairway he boomed, 'What took you so long?'"

"His monsterings were delivered with such ferocity that when I began my career as a chef at the George Hotel in Harrogate, my irascible head chef seemed almost kitten like."

Gibraltar Day, with the Lord Mayor, Victor Watson and the 2008/9 Captains

XVII MOORTOWN CENTENARY 2009

Late in 2006 the then Club Chairman, Roger Eames, asked Peter Rogerson if he would head up a centenary committee to draw up a programme of activities for the centenary year. He also invited Gerry Connolly to sit on this committee so that his vast professional experience of organizing golf events could be brought to bear. The first committee meeting took place on the 16th November 2006 with Roger, Peter, Gerry and the professional, Martin Heggie. The club chairman was of the view that a small committee would be his preferred route and he confirmed that Victor Watson had agreed to join the committee.

The general feeling was that the committee should be kept to a small hub and others approached to help as and when required, reporting back to the Centenary Committee on their progress on a regular basis. Meanwhile, the Centenary Committee would make the strategic decisions reporting back to the General Committee for ratification. In time, the centenary captain Jamie Allison, the lady captain Adele Allen, the lady secretary Ailsa Jarvis and Geoff Talbott, the press officer, together with varying event organizers attended the meetings. With a change of office of the club chairman, David Sheret, took over Roger Eames' role, as liaison between the committees.

The centenary committee drew up an ambitious programme of events which were then sifted by the general committee and a selective list of events approved. It was agreed that the launch date would be the 11th January, 2009 with a flag raising ceremony to coincide with the date of the club's formation. However, Victor Watson proposed that the celebrations should begin earlier to mark the creation of the Gibraltar hole which had been created in 2008 in advance of the full course.

Budgets and a proposed timetable were presented to the main committee and formally approved. It was decided that members would be co-opted to organize and run the various individual events with Gerry Connolly and Peter Rogerson assuming responsibility for the Centenary Festival Week, and in particular the week's two showpiece events, the Ryder Cup Reunion Pro-Am and the International Club event.

The Final Programme Of Events

01/10/2008	Gibraltar Day Centenary
11/01/2009	Flag Raising Ceremony & Cocktail Party
22/02/2009	Captain's & Past Captains' Drive in
25/04/2009	Murder at the Ryder Cup 1929
13/05/2009	Centenary Day at the Races
15/05/2009	Brabazon Trophy 15th - 17th May
24/05/2009	Ryder Cup Captain's & Past Captains' Golf and Dinner
28/06/2009	Mixed Social Golf Barbeque and Centenary Pageant
29/06/2009	Ryder Cup Reunion Pro-am & Gala Dinner
30/06/2009	International Club Invitational Event
01/07/2009	Ladies Centenary Invitation Golf & Dinner
02/07/2009	Mens Members' Day & Dinner
03/07/2009	Sporting Luncheon & Trick Shot Artist
04/07/2009	Centenary Captain's Day & Centenary Ball
31/12/2009	New Year's Eve Centenary Dance & firework display

GIBRALTAR DAY
Wednesday, October 1st, 2008

What's the connection between one of the world's most famous holes and the world's most famous motor car? The answer: both share the same birthday. Moortown's Gibraltar, the first to have been built on the course, was completed in 1908 and the first Model T Ford rolled off the production line on October 1st 1908.

With that in mind, Moortown's former president, Victor Watson, organised a double centenary party at the famous hole at which the guest-of-honour was a sparkling Model T. Members, resplendent in costumes from the turn of the century, gathered round the tee and were joined by the Lord Mayor of Leeds, Frank Robinson.

The other "T", however, didn't quite make it. Within sight of the celebrations, the truck carrying the historic car became immovably bogged down in the sodden ground of a nearby fairway.

Nothing daunted, the show continued; led by the centenary captain, Jamie Allison, the club chairman, David Sheret, and the Lord Mayor, members using hickory clubs typical of the early 1900s tried their hand at a hole-in-one competition with a new car as the prize. But the 100-year-old par-3 hole resisted all their efforts – an outcome that would doubtless have satisfied its designer, Dr Alister MacKenzie, who coincidentally was later to develop a passion for owning American automobiles.

Spectators and well-wishers with Gibraltar in the background

FLAG RAISING CEREMONY AND COCKTAIL PARTY
Sunday, January 11th, 2009

On an inhospitable and windy day in January many members availed themselves of the club's hospitality at a cocktail party when the vice captain elect, Jack Cooke, helped raise the new flag to launch the centenary year. As the year got under way in earnest, most watched from the comfort of the mixed lounge where they participated in a raffle for an elegantly framed centenary montage.

Vice Captain, Jack Cooke and the Professional Martin Heggie raising the centenary flag

Members and friends in the mixed lounge

Martin Cooper talking to Jack Cook

Centenary Flag Inauguration

Standing, left to right: Moortown Ladies with the Captain, the Centenary Captain and Vice Captain and below, 3rd and 4th from the left, the Ladies Captain and Centenary Captain

CENTENARY CAPTAIN'S DRIVE IN
Sunday, February 22nd, 2009

On a bright, sunny, but bitterly cold day, Moortown Golf Club assembled a past captains' Centenary Hall of Fame to mark the drive in of the club's centenary captain, Jamie Allison. Led by the captain to the accompaniment of a Scottish piper, twenty one former captains (including the new captain's father) paraded from the clubhouse to the first tee. There they took their places to form a unique and historic backdrop to the drive in. Dating back to the early 70s and decked out in their past captains' ties, they were announced individually to the gallery of spectators and most went on to play a shot themselves. The Captain also re-raised the centenary flag highlighting 100 years of Moortown. After the ceremony the members repaired to the bar to fortify themselves with drinks and canapés provided by the past captains, while the captain, the vice captain, the president, the lady captain and the professional played the traditional two holes to be greeted on their return by the members and the piper on the 18th green.

A group of past captains give Vice President David Roberts something to smile about

A piper marks the start of the Past Captains' Parade

The outgoing captain Bob Seaton presents the Centenary Captain Jamie Allison with his Captain's Tie

The Centenary Captain, Jamie Allison, driving in

The arrival at the parade of a past captain, Eddie Binks, under the watchful eye of the Centenary President, Brian Robinson

Twelve of the twenty-one past captains with the Lady Captain, Vice Captain and President looking on

Piping in the Past Captains

MURDER AT THE 1929 RYDER CUP
Saturday, April 25th, 2009

Moortown Golf Club's dining room was the scene for enacting one of history's fictitious but appropriately named dastardly deeds – "Murder at the Ryder Cup", the victim being one of the caddies who had met his end in the TV room. A troop of actors and actresses playing the part of various Ryder Cup players, wives and friends joined members for dinner and sought to establish their innocence with their alibis. As the dinner progressed, so the plot unwound while various tables sought to identify the perpetrator whose identity was finally revealed as the dinner came to an end.

The Lady Captain, Adele Allen, with Alma Rostron and Julie Ballantyne

The corpse in the ladies' lounge

The assembled company, suitably attired

Didi Powers with two of the actresses

The Captain, Lady Captain, and the principal actor

CENTENARY DAY AT THE RACES
Wednesday, May 13th, 2009

More than 220 members and friends assembled at the Ebor Suite at York Races to wine and dine on the Wednesday of the May Festival. The setting for Moortown's Race Day, organised by Clive Bowyer, was an exclusive dining room and balcony overlooking the course. Such was the scale of the members' support that the club was able to sponsor the 4.55 race, a 1m 2½f Class 4 race called "The Moortown Golf Club Centenary Stakes." The Captain and Lady Captain presented the prizes to the winning owners of "Barwell Bridge" and a bottle of Moortown Centenary Champagne to the winning jockey, James Doyle. While one lucky diner at the Ilkley Golf Club table had a significant win on the first race, reports of Moortown members beating the bookies were few and far between.

Geoff Mortimer amongst the ladies

Alison Mowat and Moortown's photograher Stewart Laws

Rodney Foster, Gerry Connolly and Don MacLennan

The Captain, Jamie Allison, and the Lady Captain, Adele Allen, presenting the winners' prizes

Clive Bowyer at the Ilkley Golf Club Table

RYDER CUP CAPTAIN AND PAST CAPTAINS' GOLF AND DINNER

Saturday, May 23rd and Sunday, May 24th, 2009

Jamie Ortiz Patiño, the founder and President of Valderrama Golf Club, was the principal honoured guest at this golfing weekend designed to share some special memories of Moortown and its hospitality with captains of fellow Ryder Cup host clubs, including the Honourable Company of Edinburgh Golfers, Royal Birkdale, Southport and Ainsdale, Royal Lytham, Walton Heath, Ganton, Valderrama and Celtic Manor. The event began with a Saturday evening champagne reception followed by a black tie dinner. Following a brief speech of welcome by the Captain, Moortown's former professional, Bryon Hutchinson, proposed a toast to "The Ryder Cup". The following day's golf took the form of a shotgun fourball competition with each club being paired with two Moortown past captains followed by a carvery lunch and prize presentation.

Left to right: Bob Seaton, Stuart Ritter and Steve Hennah from Celtic Manor with David Sheret

Left to right: Roger Eames, Stuart Johnson and Ian Douglas from Ganton with Peter Rogerson

David Sheret and Jamie Patino from Valderrama Golf Club

The Ryder Cup Host Clubs' Captains and Past Captains gather on the putting green before dinner

SOCIAL GOLF BARBEQUE AND CENTENARY PAGEANT
Sunday June 28th, 2009

The first event held at the Centenary Marquee was a social event consisting of 9 holes of golf followed by an outdoor barbecue provided by the in-house caterers, John and Lorraine Alexander. However, the gathering of 220 members and guests attending the event, organised by Malcolm and Jane Slinger, was considerably more than the pre-booked list and extra but unprepared tables in the Marquee had to be quickly pressed into service. After the barbeque, Victor Watson and Jane Slinger took to the stage to present one of Victor's thespian masterpieces. Magnificently cast by Victor, the production made good use of the hitherto unsuspected dramatic skills of the captain and lady captain and harnessed the talents of a number of well-known Moortown members. The Centenary Festival was thus well under way and the bar was tested well into the night.

The barbeque and bar in full swing

The Captain, Elizabeth Prust, Chris Lord, Jo Lord, Frank Prust

Pageant performers, Fiona Stoddard, Didi Powers, Shona Emmett, Angela Gault, Ian Watt, Jack Cooke.

The club chef, John Alexander, and David Kilgarriff

Dining tables were at a premium

Phil Kane serving Gail Monnickendam at the bar

The cast taking their curtain call.

RYDER CUP REUNION PRO-AM AND GALA DINNER
Monday, June 29th, 2009

More than 20 former Ryder Cup players gathered at Moortown for this the signature event in the centenary calendar. In late 2008 they had been individually invited to a reunion marking the 80th anniversary of the Ryder Cup at Moortown and the Club's 100th anniversary. Simultaneously invitations were despatched to corporate companies to a Sponsors' Night at which details of the event would be presented. Any nagging concerns about the effect of the recession were quickly dispelled and the team spots were subscribed in full that night.

Meanwhile Gerry Connolly, who spearheaded the event, secured the services of Neil Coles, the longstanding chairman of the European Tour, as the event's co-host. To bring the event to a wider public, negotiations also took place with William Hunt of the Trilby Tour, who was able to arrange Sky Sports television coverage. Discussions took place, too, with Marketing Leeds and Leeds City College who came on board as the principal sponsors. Come the big day, the teams assembled at 8.30 a.m. on a gloriously sunny morning for a champagne brunch in the marquee while the Ryder Cup players had their own reunion breakfast. Outside, 32 gleaming golf

John Jacobs and Neil Coles sharing a joke

Martin and Karen Duffield, Craig Conley, Mike and Marie West, Peter Wilson and Steve Trutch

Jazz band serenading the players at the pre-dinner drinks reception

Assistant Professional Craig Helliwell at John Jacob's Clinic

Tommy Horton winner of the Ryder Cup Shootout

Neil Coles and John Jacobs being interviewed by Dougie Donnelly

buggies awaited the teams. Prepared immaculately by Mike West and emblazoned with the team names, the buggies were laid out across the 18th fairway with 64 caddies in attendance. Fortunes rose and fell throughout the day but the eventual winning team was the Leeds legal practice of JB Law Solicitors. After the competition the Ryder Cup Players took part in a competition of their own: a Ryder Cup Shootout for Sky Sports in front of the 18th green which was won by Tommy Horton. In the evening, teams and guests assembled for a cocktail reception and Gala Dinner during which the winners and their tour pro David Good were presented with their prizes and the Ryder Cup players presented with a memento of the occasion. Afterwards the MC Dougie Donnelly conducted a televised interview with Neil Coles and John Jacobs together with the former Australian player and TV commentator Jack Newton. Afterwards, Neil and John were presented with a mounted photograph signed by the players. In turn, Neil Coles presented the captain with a magnificent gold replica of the Ryder Cup on behalf of the PGA. The memorable day concluded with a magnificent firework display provided by Moortown's own incendiary maestro, David Sayers.

Neil Coles presents the replica Ryder Cup to the Captain, Jamie Allison

The Ryder Cup players at their presentation

Replica Ryder Cup presented by the PGA

INTERNATIONAL CLUB INVITATIONAL EVENT
Tuesday, June 30th, 2009

Two Moortown teams acquitted themselves well in the week's other headline event, an am-am International Club Competition for which Moortown's ladies in turn-of-the-century costume were at hand to assist the club teams which came from six nations: including Royal Melbourne of Australia; Cork, Castle, Dun Laoghaire and Delgany in Ireland; Muirfield, the home of the Honourable Company of Edinburgh Golfers; Pinheiros Altos and San Lorenzo in Portugal, Celtic Manor in Wales and, among the English clubs, The Wentworth Club, Fairhaven, Fulford, Alwoodley, Huddersfield, St George's Hill. Again following the champagne brunch, 32 polished golf buggies awaited the teams emblazoned with team names and a Welcome message, laid out across the 18th fairway with caddies in attendance. Peter Jaggard was again controlling the live scoreboard. The event was won by Celtic Manor on 86 points – just one ahead of the second and third placed teams of Moortown's Steve Mardon's Team and the Captain's Team, led by Jamie Allison. After the competition, the teams enjoyed their own presentation dinner in the marquee with Peter Rogerson welcoming the clubs and Alistair Low, the captain of the Hon. Co. of Edinburgh Golfers, toasting Moortown. Light relief was brought to the evening by the guest speaker, Steve Tandy.

Moortown Lady Club Hosts in their Edwardian outfits

International flags behind the 18th green

The buggies lined up on the 18th fairway

Peter Rogerson in person and on the big screen welcomes the teams at the International Club event

LADIES CENTENARY INVITATION GOLF AND DINNER
Wednesday, July 1st, 2009

Moortown's famous Gibraltar had to mount its second "hole in one" defence in the centenary year when 138 ladies checked in for this 4 ball better ball Stableford competition. Awaiting them on the 9th green was a perfectly pitched prize: a one-carat diamond courtesy of the hole sponsor, David Share. One competitor came tantalisingly close to the pin, but at the end of the day, Gibraltar repulsed the best efforts of all the ladies and the diamond remained firmly out of bounds in the sponsor's safe.

Moortown's men did their bit for the day, managing the car parking, the halfway house and - the first surprise of the day - a buggy loaded with champagne and strawberries. "Such a wonderful touch on a hot sunny day," observed the Lady Captain, Adele Allen. Later the number of ladies swelled to 225 for a buffet supper preceded by drinks on the terrace. Four of Moortown's gentlemen members, in black tie order, served the canapés before the ladies filed off for their official photograph in front of the clubhouse. On their return another surprise awaited them when the band struck up and the black-tied waiters produced the Moortown version of the Full Monty. It certainly livened up the evening, though the Lady Captain's observations on their performance have not been vouchsafed to us.

The buffet and further entertainment from a magician was followed by the formal prize giving during which the President of Yorkshire, Brenda Parker, presented Adele Allen with a Yorkshire Centenary Plate which she accepted on behalf of the Ladies. The main prize of the day was won by the only international team to enter: Jo Lord of Moortown, Liz Cooper from Royal Melbourne and Susan Russell and Denise Reed, both from Portugal's Pineros Altos, scoring 91 points. The evening concluded with a Frank Sinatra tribute band which gave the girls the opportunity to dance away the final hours of the evening after a long but fun-packed day at which all were able to "Enjoy the Memory". In addition the day raised £2,000 for the Lady Captain's chosen charity, Breast Cancer Research.

Linda Burrows Ilkley Golf Club; Brenda Parker YLCGA President, Julie Robinson Headingley Golf Club and the Centenary Lady Captain, Adele Allen

Liz Boldy and Vicky Renny with guests at the Terrace Champagne Reception

Sue Winn's party at the Dinner

David Share sponsored a Hole in One at the 10th for a 1 Carat Diamond

MENS MEMBERS' DAY AND DINNER
Thursday, July 2nd, 2009

Entry to this tournament and the dinner that followed came free-of-charge and it was quickly oversubscribed. Martin Heggie, who sponsored and organised the event, promptly added a further morning shotgun to the planned lunchtime shotgun in order to accommodate the extra members. A selection of winners is shown here. Martin organised a hypnotist Kris von Sponneck for the after-dinner entertainment and soon many members were laid out inert on the floor or carrying out the hypnotist's every command.

Left to right:
Anthony Burrows, Peter Fearnley, the Captain, Rory Wilson

Left to right:
Fred Davies, Paul Fullerton, the Captain, Malcolm Slinger

Left to right: Paul Carrigill, Mark Lofthouse, the Captain, Duncan and David McCarthy

Left to right: Bob Seaton, Richard Hurst, the Captain, Mike Cooper, Bob Timmis

Left to right: Jonathan Greenwood, Richard Cooper, the Captain, Simon Roberts, Robert Treweek

Chris Lord and Jamie Chappell enjoying the entertainment

Martin Heggie and the hostess making the draw

Down and out under hypnosis

SPORTSMAN'S LUNCHEON AND TRICK SHOT ARTIST
Friday, July 3rd, 2009

250 members and guests turned out for this event which took place on the only day of the Festival week when the weather was not sunny; torrential rain prevented the 'trick shot golf' going ahead as planned before lunch. But the event organiser, Geoff Mortimer, quickly re-jigged the timetable, postponing the trick shot event to after lunch while bringing on early the girl band "Heavenly" to open the proceedings and bringing forward the lunch. The Liverpool comedian, Willie Miller, proved a highly popular turn after which, happily, the rain stopped in time for Dave Edwards' impressive exhibition of trick shots.

Geoff Mortimer with the Lunch Hostesses

Geoff Mortimer briefing Willie Miller before the event

David Edwards sitting down to it

Moortown's Assistant Pros: Craig Helliwell teeing up from Eddie Hammond's mouth

David Edwards using a long wood

David Edwards on the high tees

David Edwards teeing up using Craig Helliwell

David Edwards firing a ball through a block of wood

CENTENARY CAPTAIN'S DAY AND CENTENARY BALL
Saturday, July 4th, 2009

The Centenary Captain, Jamie Allison, concluded the week with the traditional Captain's Day Golf Day which was marked by a return of the sunshine, a full field of competitors and the time-honoured warm welcome at the 'half-way house'. The conclusion of the golf was followed by the equally traditional rush to get into black tie order for the evening dinner and formal member's photographs which preceded it. The after-dinner dancing took place to the strains of the curiously named Big J and the Piccolo Chickens Band and the evening concluded with yet another magnificent firework display provided by David Sayers.

Left to right: Paul Turner, Adrian Hinchcliffe, Richard Pennington, Eddie Winn, Robert Treweek, Simon Roberts

Mr and Mrs Steve Downes and Mr and Mrs Tom Adams

Left to right: Martin and Jackie Waide, John Murtland, Pauline and Alan Davenport

The Centenary Ball Cocktail Reception

Left to right: Peter Holmes, Ian and Anne Chippindale, Graham Etherington, Ian Esplin, Bill Dales

Left to right: John Lawson-Brown, Linda Hudson and Vince Green

*Back row left to Right: Jonathan Flint, Mike McCarthy, Andy Croston,
Front row left to right: Jeff Flint and Terry Telford*

*Left to Right: Clive Bowyer, Lady Captain Adele Allen, Nick Moore,
Bob Timmis, Robert Winterton, David Marriott*

Fred Lawson-Brown, T J (Pa) Braime, Billy Lord, Herbert Sutcliffe and Richard Lawson-Brown

XVIII OFFICERS OF THE CLUB

CAPTAINS

A key office at every golf club is that of the club captain. In the early days of Moortown, the process of nomination was shrouded in mystery, but the committee was always able to propose an appropriate nominee. After 1923 the election of a captain was on the basis of a nomination from the General Committee to be confirmed at the next Annual General Meeting. The office of Vice-Captain did not exist, but in 1945 there was much debate amongst members on the methods used for the selection of the Captain and the need to introduce the office of Vice-Captain. A sub-committee of Messrs Alcock, Eley, and Lawson-Brown was set up to recommend a recognised procedure to be adopted in the selection of nominations for the offices of captain and vice-captain. It recommended that a panel consisting of the existing captain, his two immediate predecessors and the vice-captain should select a suitable candidate for captain. If the name did not meet with the approval of the General Committee, the panel would submit a further nomination. Any nomination could come from the general body of members as long as it was in accordance with the club regulations. The Captain was then selected at the next Annual General Meeting. The sub-committee agreed on the need for a vice-captain and proposed that the vice-captain should automatically succeed to the office of captain.

This procedure was adopted and followed until 1960 when it was decided that the nominations for vice-captain, president and vice-presidents should be made at a meeting of a General Committee sub-committee consisting of the captain and all past-captains who were still members.

The captain traditionally drives in on the Sunday after the AGM with the President, the Vice Captain, and the Professional.

CAPTAINS

Year	Name	Year	Name	Year	Name
1909-10	F.J. Turner	1948	W. Lord	1979	K.M. Baldwin
1911	J.F. White	1949	J.W. Kidd	1980	D. Jones
1912	C.W. Collier	1950	S. Bolton	1981	E. Binks
1913	Dr A. MacKenzie	1951	H. Turner	1982	G. Kitchingman
1914	R. Pegler	1952	L.E. Barrett	1983	C.R. Langley
1915	A.P. Bland	1953	C. Atkinson	1984	R.J. Parker
1916-19	R.H. Robey	1954	R. Lawson-Brown	1985	R. Hunt
1920	F.J.F. Curtis	1955	F.M. Wilson	1986	M.J. Riley
1921	S.R. Rush	1956	H. Sutcliffe	1987	T. O'Hara
1922	E. Stockdale	1957	A.B. Sharman	1988	J. Boyd
1923	T. Child	1958	F.J. Brown	1989	D. Roberts
1924	J. Greenwood	1959	P.N. Pound	1990	A.G. Parker
1925-26	J.A. Sykes	1960	R.B. Hopkins	1991	P.B. Stevenson
1927	W. Power	1961	C.C. Hodgson	1992	B. Robinson
1928	S.G. Hobbs	1962	A. Turner	1993	D.F. Allison
1929	A. Green	1963	R.H. Hunt	1994	D.R.W. Lodge
1930	J.F. White	1964	A.R. Alvin	1995	V. Green
1931	F. Lawson-Brown	1965	H.F. Graham	1996	P.M. Rogerson
1932	J.R. Benley	1966	R.E. Robinson	1997	Dr D.A. Hanley
1933	N. Hurtley	1967	J.R. Burrows	1998	M.E. Craven
1934	T.F. Braime	1968	R.M. Hockin	1999	M. Tain
1935	E. Alcock	1969	B.H.J. Thompson	2000	J.R. Eames
1936	H. Wyndham West	1970	D.I.D. Blackburn	2001	G.G. Mortimer
1937	W. C. Beverley	1971	W.H. King	2002	C.J. Craven
1938	B.S. Lister	1972	B.I. Wilson	2003	N.A. Watt
1939-42	E. White	1973	A.G.S. Grant	2004	D.J. MacLennan
1943	S. Grove	1974	A.W. Hockin	2005	J.D. Flint
1944	G. Eley	1975	G.C. Robson	2006	C. C. Bowyer
1945	A. Boult	1976	V.H. Watson	2007	D. R. Sheret
1946	E. Penfold	1977	J.M. Guyatt	2008	R. A. Seaton
1947	C.J. Rhodes	1978	A.C. Clues	2009	J. R. F. Allison

Alan Turner, Alan Grant, Ian Wilson and Bryon Hutchinson

1960 Captain Ronald Hopkins with J W Foreman (Margaret calvert's Father) Laurie Barrett and Alf Sharman

1984 Captain Roland Parker driving in

1990 Captain Albert Parker driving in

1954 Past Captains Charlie Rhodes, Charlie Atkinson and Harry Turner

1978 Arthur Clues Drive-in with Paul Johnson, Frank Brown and Ken Baldwin

Opening of New Course - R J Parker Chairman, A Turner President, D Roberts Captain, R Brown Secretary, S Sinclair Captain R&A, A Parker Vice Captain and B Hutchinson Professional

PRESIDENTS

1910-34	Hon. Rupert E. Beckett	1982-84	P. N. Pound
		1985-87	A. W. Hockin
1935-54	T. F. Braime	1988-90	A. Turner
1955	F. Lawson-Brown	1991-93	E. Binks
1956-66	J. A. Sykes	1994-96	D. Jones
1967-69	H. Turner	1997-99	V. H. Watson
1970-72	R. B. Hopkins	2000-02	R. J. Parker
1973-75	L. E. Barrett	2003-05	T O'Hara
1976-78	F. J. Brown	2006-08	J M Guyatt
1979-81	A. B. Sharman	2009	B Robinson

PRESIDENTS

In the early days the office of president was occupied by the Hon. Rupert Beckett but in 1956 it was suggested that the office of president should not be held for more than three years, a proposal which was implemented that year on the retirement of J Arthur Sykes. Each year the gentlemen and the ladies play for their respective President Prizes, a tradition which has been maintained since the foundation.

2009 Centenary President Brian Robinson

CHAIRMEN

Year	Name	Year	Name
1909	Dr A. MacKenzie	1968-69	P.N. Pound
1910	F.J. Turner	1970-72	V.H. Watson
1911	J.F. White	1973-75	A. Turner
1912	S.R. Rush	1976-78	E.N. Pullan
1915-25	L. Moore	1979-82	R.J. Parker
1926-44	T.F. Braime	1983-85	E. Binks
1945	N. Hurtley	1986-89	R.J. Parker
1946-49	E. Alcock	1990-98	T. O'Hara
1950-58	R.B. Hopkins	1999-01	P.M. Rogerson
1959-63	R. Learmonth	2002-07	J.R. Eames
1964-65	L.E. Barrett	2008	D. Sheret
1966-67	R.H. Hunt		

SECRETARIES

Year	Name	Year	Name
1909-10	J.N. Casson	1962-64	J.C. Reid
1911-29	J.F. White	1964-70	J.R. Collinge
1929-33	J. Lawson-Brown	1971	G.J.B. Hogg
1934-38	W. Harrap	1971-78	R. Cartwright
1940	S. Grove	1978-80	B.H.J. Thompson
1941-45	C.J. Rhodes	1981	P.N. Pound
1946-49	W.H. McMinn	1981-86	K.M. Baldwin
1950-	Brig E.A. Moreton	1987	K. Symons
1951-55	C.J. Rhodes	1987-92	R.H. Brown
1955	R.W.M. Hall	1993-97	T. Hughes
1956	A. Jones	1998-00	C.A. Moore
1957	L.E. Barrett	2000-05	K.C. Bradley
1958-59	L.E. Barrett	2005-07	J.L. Hall
1960	J.C. Reid	2007	R.S.G. Limbert
1961	Wg Com. J.R. Pullan		

TREASURERS

Year	Name	Year	Name
1909	F.J. Turner	1967-69	R.A. Calvert
1910-22	J.A. Preston	1970	G.J.B. Hogg
1923-34	N. Hurtley	1971	G.K. Day
1932-34	A.H. Whalley	1972-76	J.M. Kaye
1935-50	S. Grove	1977-79	R.S. Buckle
1950	C.J. Rhodes	1980-83	J.S. Battye
1951-52	F.W. Foreman	1984-99	J.C. Murtland
1953-55	C.J. Dixon	2000	D. Mann
1956-58	R. Learmonth	2001-05	G. Gibson
1959-60	T.H.C. Hobbs	2005-08	L. Fawke
1961-63	S.J. Warnes	2009-	A. Marshall
1964-66	W.W. McInley		

CHAIRMEN (GENERAL COMMITTEE)

The club chairman is elected annually by the full committee from within the membership of that committee on its formation. By tradition this election is held on the first Monday following the AGM and so the new or re-elected chairman is therefore a figure who has been elected by the whole club.

Sub Committee Chairman are elected annually by the full committee with the chairman presiding. The chairman, like the captain and vice captain, sit on all sub committees.

SECRETARIES

A full-time secretary had been appointed in 1934 at an annual salary of £200. But five years later he resigned when the club decided it could no longer afford his services and instead reverted to its previous practice: paying an honorarium to a selected member. The Committee has tried similar appointments in later years but the staying power of those appointed has not been impressive. What can it be about Moortown and its members that only fellow members on an honorarium seem to last the distance?

TREASURERS

The role of treasurer has always been a thankless one, with pressures to manage the finances of the club as well as the presentation of the accounts at the AGM to the members, who have many varying financial views. In recent times mention must be made of the great commitment made to the club by John Murtland, one of the longest-standing treasurers, who held the office for 15 years from 1984 to 1999.

2002 – 2007 Chairman Roger Eames

2000 – 2005 Secretary Ken Bradley, Barry Corscadden and Captain Malcom Tain

1984 – 1999 Treasurer John Murtland

Rhododendrons by the 18th Tee

XIX FAUNA AND FLORA

If the club's founders of 1909 could walk the Moortown of 2009, they would, of course, see some huge changes in the natural history of their course. At its most obvious, they would see how heavily wooded it has become. But they would see, too, that the Moortown of today remains very much a heathland course with flora and fauna to match. Its 1909 title of Black Moor was an apt description.

Typically for heathland with its peaty and often boggy conditions is heather in profusion together with gorse and broom. Introduced species can be found in the parkland sections of the course but natural heather has been at Moortown in abundance right from the start.

Unusually there are three types of heather on the course; Ling with its lilac flowers is the most common but there is also Bell with its characteristic big purplish-red flowers as well as the cross-leaved variety with pink flowers. Natural though it is to the area, there has been some management of the heather's growth by the club's greens staff. Heather seed has been harvested by them for planting elsewhere on the course, thus increasing the spread and range of this attractive feature.

Moreover, it is a characteristic of heather to produce a seed bank from its fallen seeds. They can lie dormant for many years – even decades - beneath layers of built up vegetation from leaves and grass. Peeling back this organic matter allows the seeds to regenerate and thus heather returns to areas in which it has been lost over the years. Again, the club has taken advantage of this technique in its husbandry of the historic heather.

There is a diverse range of grasses which include the rye and meadow species in the parkland areas through to the fescues, bents, wavy hair and purple moor grass more common in the heathland areas.

One of Moortown's most explosively colourful features has been its vast spread of rhododendrons which over the years have flourished and grown vigorously in the acidic peaty soil. As a result management and reduction have been required in order to keep them in proportion. However, when the blooms are at their best, one of the most dramatic sights is the continuous line of rhododendrons which flank the length of the 18th fairway. Other introduced species include some majestic azaleas as well as ornamental laurel.

Moortown's wild flowers include swathes of bluebells in the woods. Elsewhere there is meadowsweet, knapweed, herb willow, foxgloves, yarrow, harebells and flag irises.

One of the most significant influences on the nature of the course has been the outward spread of building developments in Leeds and its outskirts. Once surrounded by farmland, Moortown is now surrounded by housing whose arrival some years ago threatened to impact heavily on the aesthetics of the course. In some measure these issues prompted the Green Committee to undertake a programme of tree and shrub planting. Birch was indigenous to the landscape and, by regeneration, had already established copses on the course. The peaty nature of the soil encouraged the planting of rhododendron bushes, but in 1951 and 1953 a large number of pine trees were obtained from Fewston for planting on the first, fifth, sixth and seventeenth holes. Firs were also planted along the second fairway and by the side of the fourteenth green. As these plantings matured, so the effect on the landscape and the character of the golf course was significant. Recently there has been some thinning out of the trees but there are many fine examples of Scots Pine, silver birch, beech, rowan and oak.

Heather on the 4th hole

Arguably the most unusual addition to Moortown's landscape was the gift of an American Red Oak Tree from Oak Hill Club in Rochester, New York. Sandy Jones, the PGA chief executive, presented it to Moortown with a plaque and certificate at the club's Annual Dinner in November 2001 in recognition of Moortown's staging of the 1929 Ryder Cup. The sapling was planted first alongside the 7th fairway but was later moved to its current position on the left on the approach to Gibraltar. Aerial photographs taken in 2009 of the course's individual holes shown in the book clearly illustrate the highly-wooded nature of the course today.

Also looking down on Moortown's acres, have been the most recent and easily the most spectacular of its wildlife features. Red kites with their two-metre wingspan – are regular visitors to the course from their nesting places just north of Moortown on the Harewood Estate where they were introduced in a breeding programme in 1999. At lower levels golfers have often surprised pheasants taking cover in the rough, presumably refugees from nearby shoots. Deer can also be spotted from time to time. Far less shy, however, are the foxes on the course, including one particularly bold family which periodically appeared on the terrace outside the clubhouse to peer through windows.

Red Oak at Gibraltar

Pheasant near the ditch on the 16th hole

Harewood Red Kite, 2008

Rhododendrons on the 18th fairway

Yellow Azalea Bush at the 18th tee

Azeleas at the 10th tee at the half way house

XX WHAT THE PLAYERS SAY

A number of the players have been kind enough to send congratulatory letters for our Centenary. We are pleased to reproduce a selection from some of the worlds' leading players.

The Captain,
Moortown Golf Club,
Harrogate Road
Leeds,
LS17 7DB

Dear Captain,

I am writing to thank you for the most wonderful day I enjoyed at the Club on Monday 29th of June.

Everything about the day gave me so much pleasure, seeing so many old friends, re-living past involvements with the Club, renewing life-long acquaintances with Neil Coles, Jack Newton etc etc. Neil has been such a great player, and still is, but as the long-serving Chairman of the European Tour, his leadership has been very much part of the huge success of the European Tour.

On a personal basis to include my daughter Joanna who, like me, was thrilled to be with Pam and Aubrey Phillipson, dear friends over many, many years.

The welcome which was extended to all of we visitors, was so very heartwarming. The most generous hospitality along with all the arrangements pro-am, interviews, including the timing of all the different activities, was simply superb. To top it all, my lovely silver money-clip, which will serve to remind me of such a perfect day. Jo and I are so grateful to have been part of it. Please pass on to all concerned, how much we appreciated this wonderful occasion.

Very Sincerely,

John Jacobs.

John Jacobs

COLIN MONTGOMERIE

1 June 2009

Jamie Allison
Centenary Captain
The Moortown Golf Club
Harrogate Road
Alwoodley
Leeds LS17 7DB

Dear Jamie

Centenary Year – The Moortown Golf Club

Sorry that due to tournament commitments I will be unable to visit Moortown in your centenary year.

I can recall playing many times at your course in my youth, living in Ilkley at the time, and I thoroughly enjoyed the course and the members that I played with. I remember playing with you and James Robson on more than one occasion !

It was also good to meet up with you, many years later, at the Forest of Arden in my capacity as a Lloyds TSB Ambassador.

Obviously the Ryder Cup is a very special event to me especially having the honour as Captain this year, and to think that the club that hosted the very first UK match, which we won !, is now 100 years old is quite special.

Many congratulations to you and your members, and I hope you have a fantastic year. If I am passing through Leeds at any point this year, I will try and call in to see you all.

Kind regards.

Yours sincerely,

Colin Montgomerie

Colin Montgomerie
McCormack House
Burlington Lane
London W4 2TH

T: +44 (0)20 8233 5030
F: +44 (0)20 8233 5268

jane.brooks@imgworld.com
www.colinmontgomerie.com

PETER ALLISS - GOLF LIMITED

**MOORTOWN GOLF CLUB
CENTENARY CELEBRATIONS 2009**

As the years go by many more clubs celebrate their centenary, but there's always an air of excitement when the 100 year barrier is broken. This is certainly the case with the Moortown Golf Club, which has been a part of my life for seventy years.

When my father was professional at the Temple Newsam Golf Club in the mid-1930s I remember him talking in glowing terms about the enjoyment he'd had playing the course, and then later, when I was doing my National Service in 1949, I learnt of its delights for myself.

There were many tournaments played there during my career as a tournament golfer and when I was professional at the Moor Allerton Golf Club, visits to the course for various competitions, alliances and pro-ams, the cosiness of the club house, and the pro shop looking out on a very attractive putting green, all added to the wonder and mystique of Moortown Golf Club.

Long may you continue.

Peter Alliss

PO Box 224, Hindhead, Surrey GU26 6WQ · TELEPHONE 01428 607253 · FAX 01428 607843
E-MAIL jackie@alliss-promotions.co.uk or (Roy Cooper) - roy@allissgolf.co.uk
REGISTERED OFFICE 1 CONDUIT ST. LONDON W1S 2XA · VAT NO 733 4212 64 · INCORPORATED IN THE UNITED KINGDOM NO 2193981

TOM WATSON
1901 WEST 47TH PLACE • SUITE 200 • WESTWOOD, KANSAS 66205
TEL: 913-432-1020   FAX: 913-432-9966

Mr. Jamie Allison
Moortown Golf Club
Harrogate Road
Alwoodley
Leeds LS17 7DB

Dear Mr. Allison,

In 1976, as the reigning Open Champion, I was invited to play with the Club's Captain, Victor Watson, in a match play called "The Watsons v the Rest of the World."

As a result, I was able to see at first hand and play the 1929 Ryder Cup Course which had been designed by the famous Dr. Alister MacKenzie.

I have happy memories of that day and of meeting the Moortown members and I wish them much success for their centenary and hope they have a year to remember.

Sincerely,

Tom Watson

Jack Nicklaus

January 1, 2009

To The Members of the Moortown Golf Club:

There is a wonderful kinship enjoyed among golfers the world over. We share not only a love for the game itself, but a reverence for its history and a commitment to its preservation. Thus, it gives me special pleasure to offer my best wishes and congratulations as you observe Moortown Golf Club's 100th Anniversary.

As members of this special club, you have promoted the sportsmanship and camaraderie of the game for decades and have proudly passed those fundamentals along from generation to generation. On this special occasion, my thanks and compliments go to each of you for carrying on these traditions. You are gracious ambassadors for the game we love.

Congratulations once again and best wishes for the next hundred years.

Sincerely,

Jack Nicklaus

Moortown Golf Club Limited
Harrogate Road
Alwoodley
Leeds LS17 7DB
West Yorkshire
United Kingdom

11780 U. S. Highway # 1, Suite 500, North Palm Beach, Florida 33408

Ian Woosnam
European Ryder Cup Captain

11th August 2009

Moortown Golf Club
Harrogate Road
Alwoodley
Leeds
LS17 7DB

To the Members of Moortown Golf Club,

Centenary Celebrations

I am writing to congratulate Moortown Golf Club on its Centenary and also the 80th Anniversary of the 1929 Ryder Cup Matches.

I have many happy memories of the course and especially remember playing with Lionel Platts and Hedley Muscroft in those early days.

Best wishes to you all. Good luck with your celebrations.

Ian Woosnam

La Hougue, La Grande Route de St Pierre, St Peter, Jersey, Channel Islands JE3 7AX
Tel: +44 (0)20 8233 5077   e-mail: dbarlow@imgworld.com   Ryder Cup Limited, Registered in England No 2662321

Standing left to right: Peter Rogerson (1996), Mike Craven (1998), Malcolm Tain (1999), Roger Eames (2000), Geoff Mortimer (2001), Chris
Seated left to right: Gerald Robson (1975), John Guyatt (1977), Eddie Binks (1981), Colin La
Jamie Allison (Centenary Captain 2009), Brian Robinson (1992), David Ro